BEYOND A REASONABLE DOUBT

BEYOND A REASONABLE DOUBT

TRUE STORIES OF AN L.A. PRIVATE EYE

EDDY L. McCLAIN CPI

Charleston, SC
www.PalmettoPublishing.com

Beyond a Reasonable Doubt
Copyright © 2022 by Eddy L. McClain CPI

First Edition

Hardcover ISBN: 979-8-8229-0012-7
Paperback ISBN: 979-8-8229-0013-4

CONTENTS

ABOUT THE BOOK ix

LOS ANGELES FIRST (AND LAST) AIR RAID 1

FLYING 5

WILD TURKEY AND WATER 9

MAYNARD HUMMEL AND ME 11

MY FIRST TRIP TO PHOENIX 15

THE STOGIE FROM SKOKIE 19

GOOD SAMARITAN HOSPITAL 23

HOWARD HUGHES AND ME 27

MURDER HE WROTE 29

FISHING WITH THE FEDS 33

THE SPYING SCIENTIST CONSPIRACY 43

DENIM Part one 45

DENIM Part two 49

MY FIRST SAILING VOYAGE 53

SAD EPILOGUE 59

THE CASE OF THE MISSING TIRES 61

CLEM 67

A CLASSIC INSURANCE DEFENSE CASE 71

THE CASE OF THE TOP SECRET PLANS 81

JASPER WILLIAM McCLAIN 89

SOUPS ON 95

AN IN-DEPTH PERSONAL INVESTIGATION 99

TAPE PIRACY   101

MY FIRST (AND LAST) KIDNAPPING INVESTIGATION   109

GETTING TO MOUNT OLYMPUS   113

RUNAWAYS #1   117

RUNAWAYS #2   119

A MYSTERY HOMICIDE   123

JAVA JAVA   125

MANY THNGS BEGIN AT THE AIRPORT   137

THE RETURN OF THE DESERT RAT   143

THE "HUSH" CASE   147

ADDING K & S SECURITY   151

U.S. BORAX STRIKE   153

HOLLYWOOD PARK RACE TRACK   159

MAYNARD HUMMEL NEEDS A JOB   161

DECATUR   163

ASPARAGUS   173

GENE AUTRY and the UNITED STATES MARINES   179

PUNITIVE DAMAGES   183

THE VINDICTIVE THIEVES   189

DEADWEIGHT EMPLOYMENT CONTRACTS   191

BEFORE THERE WAS ENRON . . . THERE WAS THIS GUY   193

BANK FRAUD   197

THE MILLION DOLLAR JUROR   199

THE GANG-BANGING DOPE DEALERS   201

KNUTE   203

MISCELLANY   207

WHY YOU NEED TO BELONG TO TRADE ASSOCIATIONS   213

HISTORY   215

As published on the August 2000 cover of PI Magazine

ABOUT THE BOOK

This eclectic book is a collection of true short stories about investigations that I have conducted over my years as a private investigator in California, including a few personal vignettes about my life and people I have known.

During the Korean War, I served stateside as a Staff Sergeant in the 508th Airborne Regimental Combat Team after completing Parachute School at Fort Benning, Georgia, and later as an instructor at the NCO Academy, Fort Campbell, Kentucky.

The United States Army is good at teaching leadership and my three years of Army learning has greatly helped my career in leading companies and organizations. I have also learned a great deal by fortunately being employed by Krout & Schneider, the very fine, now 95-year-old firm, where I have prospered.

I am a founding member and past President of CALI, the California Association of Licensed Investigators, the world's largest investigation association. I am also a past President of NCISS, the National Council of Investigation and Security Services. I have served as chairman of both association's Legislative Committees and have testified on behalf of the profession four times before Congress and numerous times in Sacramento.

EDDY L. McCLAIN CPI

LOS ANGELES FIRST (AND LAST) AIR RAID

After the crops were harvested in 1941, my parents, Irving and Dorothy left the farm near Nobleford and traveled to California for the winter. I went with them and was enrolled in a third-grade class at Richland Avenue Elementary School in West Los Angeles. I shared a desk with a girl who had asthma. We stayed with my Aunt Virginia in her home on Barrington Ave, just south of Pico, which is now under the I-10 freeway, in West Los Angeles. From her front door, you could look across the bean fields and see Douglas Aircraft about eight blocks away.

On Sunday morning, December 7, I walked to the corner of Pico and Bundy and purchased a chili dog at the Nuway hot dog stand for a quarter. A little later in the day we heard the news that Pearl Harbor had been attacked by the Japanese fleet.

The next day, President Franklin Roosevelt delivered his famous "a date that will live in infamy" speech to a joint session of Congress. My Dad Irving applied and was hired by Douglas Aircraft as a tool and die maker. He worked the graveyard shift building the Boston A-20 attack bomber. The country was in a state of panic.

The glass roof of Douglas Aircraft was painted black and all nearby homes had to be rigged for blackouts. Because L.A. was located on the West Coast, there was more concern. Anti-aircraft batteries were installed near Aunt Virginia's home to protect Douglas.

The FBI began rounding up Japanese-American citizens. On February 19, 1942, the President signed Executive Order 9066 formally authorizing the arrest of all persons of Japanese descent eventually interring 117,000 of them in camps all over the country. Even Canada, Mexico and many Central and South American countries, did so as well. Regrettably, they were not released until 1946. To say there was paranoia is an understatement. A sad chapter in American history.

This was the same period when the Canadian government seized all higher caliber rifles from legal aliens (that was us and many others) and held Irv's 30.30 in the Baron's jail until the war was over. With the jail cell full of rifles, there was no room for any Mountie (RCMP) prisoners.

On February 23, 1942, a Japanese submarine surfaced off the coast of California just North of Santa Barbara and fired 13 shells at the Tidewater Oil Refinery causing minimal damage. Paranoia increased.

On the next night, February 24, some defense workers thought they saw enemy aircraft over Los Angeles and panic spread that there was an air raid underway. The defenders opened up with anti-aircraft firing 1,440 rounds of mostly

12.8-pound shells (plus too many .50 caliber machine gun rounds to count), into the air at imaginary targets.

My Dad Irving was at work when the fusillade began and they went to total blackout at Douglas. Irv said he didn't get much work done that night. I slept through it and was one of the few kids at school the next day who didn't have a souvenir piece of shrapnel for show and tell. The Army was very embarrassed and hushed up the incident attributed to "war nerves."

My Aunt Virginia, married a fellow named Bob Boles early in the War. Uncle Bob who had been an employee of MGM Studios, was chosen by actor Clark Gable to be camera operator on Gable's B-17 crew filming recruiting films. (See Clark Gable in *Wikipedia*) The Army Air Corps thought it was good PR to have an all-MGM bomber crew. They flew several combat missions and their B-17 got shot up pretty bad with some fatalities on one bomb run over Germany. Uncle Bob also served as a waste gunner on the bomber.

FLYING

In the early forties in Alberta, Canada, the wage for a farm hand was $100 per month plus room and board. The farmer provided sleeping quarters and the worker took his meals with the family. At harvest time, which usually involved 12 to 14 hours days, wages were bumped up to $6 per day.

When I was 13, my Uncle Garland offered me a job driving tractor at harvest time pulling his old Holt combine. He paid me full man's wages of $6 per day. I saved that money and when I was 17, began taking flying lessons in Lethbridge. Lessons cost $6.50 per hour which included the plane and instructor

My first instructor was "Watty" Watts, a British former Spitfire pilot who fought in the Battle of Britain. He was a nervous little man who seemed to perspire, even on cold days. Later, I heard that he died in a crash with a student. Watts taught me the basics including doing spins which involved pulling back the stick until the plane stalled, then kicking on full left or right rudder. Both stalls and spins were scary. It was interesting how the airplane would shudder as it stalled.

After having four hours logged, it was time for my first solo in the Fleet Canuck. It was a beautiful day with only about five knots of wind. I took off and flew out to the farm and around for an hour, then back to the airport. I noticed the wind sock was pointing from west to east, but its straight-out configuration didn't register with me. I had not been taught how to do power landings, so as I approached the runway from the east, I throttled back and attempted to glide down to the runway to make a three-point landing.

When I was down to about fifty feet in the air, the plane suddenly dropped precipitously from its glide which scared me considerably so I pushed the throttle all the way and decided to go around again. This time I was gliding down nicely but when I was just about to touch down, the plane suddenly rose a bunch. So, I hit the throttle again and went around. I decided I would put it down no matter what happened. It was going nicely until the last second when the plane suddenly tilted allowing only the right wheel to jarringly hit the runway causing the right wing to barely scrape the runway.

After I had coasted to a stop, I had trouble getting the plane to turn even when I applied extra power. I couldn't figure it out. Then I realized the fire truck had pulled up alongside me with three guys on it. My instructor opened the door and told me to get out and drive the fire truck back to the hanger. That was when I realized the wind was blowing like hell and I saw each of the other two guys clamp on to a wing before the three of them walked and taxied the plane back to the hanger. My instructor mumbled something about learning power landings, which we did on my next lesson. The good old Alberta wind had come up without warning.

The man who gave the flying and classroom tests for the whole Province of Alberta only came by a few times per year. He flew the famous De Havilland Otter which is the same plane you see them flying today in Alaska on pontoons. It was seven-passenger and had a 500 horsepower Pratt and Whitney engine vs my little Fleet Canuck which was about 90 hp. A few years later I learned that he also was killed in a crash with a student.

After I obtained my Canadian pilots license, though I am American, I volunteered to be a Flying Officer for the RCAF, the Royal Canadian Air Force. At their HQ in Medicine Hat, Alberta, I was told I had passed all the tests with flying colors and only needed to pass the physical exam. This was my first exposure to the colored dots test. I flunked. My eyes were classed as "defective unsafe" for color blindness. They said they would have taken me during World War II, but they weren't losing as many pilots in Korea. They offered Radio or Navigation officer, but I declined. I was a pilot.

My friend Gaines Imeson obtained his commercial license and started flying for Trans Canada Airlines. Somewhere along the line, TCA laid him off so he started flying bush out of Quebec hauling mostly freight. One day he took off with a full load of fuel in poor weather and his last radio transmission was "the truck broke loose." They say the crash site burned for three hours.

This meant that the three pilots who were instrumental in my flying, all died in plane crashes. I wondered if this was an omen. In any event, I switched to parachute jumping for safety reasons.

When I enlisted in the Army, I volunteered for Airborne. Upon finishing basic training at Ft. Ord, the Army sent my entire training company to Korea. Because I had volunteered for Airborne, they sent me to parachute school in Georgia.

After my discharge, I enrolled at Los Angeles Harbor College on the G.I. Bill. On the first day's initial class, the instructor announced that the orientation would be given by the student body president. His name was Tachihara. I recognized him immediately as my former lieutenant platoon leader at Fort Ord. After the class I spoke to him. He didn't remember me, but informed me about what happened in Korea. Sadly, I remembered two of the four names he said didn't make it back.

If you notice, almost every general you see on TV, no matter how much other cabbage is on their chests, proudly wears airborne wings, often, master jumper wings signifying at least 65 jumps.

WILD TURKEY AND WATER

On June 17, 1953, I was driving my 1951 Ford down a long sloping curve on a Georgia two-lane highway outside of Macon when I noticed two big wild turkeys sitting just off the pavement. As I neared them, they inexplicably decide to fly across the highway. I had little room to maneuver. One made it but the other hit directly on the driver's side of my two-piece windshield. Fortunately, I was wearing sun glasses and a skipper's cap. Part of the glass was missing altogether and the rest bent in with occasional chips flying into my glasses as I headed for Macon. In town, a cop stopped me and said I shouldn't be driving around like that, but he didn't say I couldn't. So I proceeded on to my destination in South Carolina and had to blow ninety bucks the next day for a new windshield. There were feathers in all of my clothes in the back that seemed to reappear, every once in a while, for years.

Two days later I marched down the aisle with Marcia in the oldest Presbyterian church in South Carolina. It was one of two buildings, the other being the nearby First Baptist church, that Yankee General William Tecumseh Sherman spared on his famous March to the Sea in 1865 when he burned the rest of the City of Columbia, the State Capitol, to the ground. But that's another story.

The next day we drove to Fort Campbell, Kentucky, where my new 8' x 33' trailer was parked less than a mile outside the gate. The road to the trailer park was half in Kentucky and half in Tennessee. Our space was at the end of the row of about twelve spaces and also at the end of the waterline. I would rush home from work every night to try to get the soap off before the water pressure turned into a dribble.

My First Sergeant Eplin and his family lived in the park as did our friends Kepley and Hagmire who, like me, were corporals in my company. Eplin was a great First Sergeant who had made a combat jump at Normandy on D-Day, and another jump in Holland where we lost a lot of paratroopers. Hollywood made a movie about it, *THE LONGEST DAY.*

A few months later, my name came up on the waiting list for a trailer space on the base. The space rent was only $8.33 per month and included sewer, free electricity, water, and trash service once per week by prisoners from the stockade. Marcia could also watch the parachuting, from this front row location near the drop zone.

MAYNARD HUMMEL AND ME

After my discharge from the Army in 1955, and returning to California, I enrolled in college on the GI Bill. We borrowed some money and leased a motel at 83rd Street and Figueroa (currently the neighborhood of the Eight Trey Crips gang). The idea was to rent rooms at night and I would attend school during the day.

A few months later the doorbell rang. It was a flying buddy from Canada named Hans Reich. Hans spoke fluent German so the Canadian Army used him to interrogate Germans during WWII. Now he was back to farming in Alberta.

I offered him a drink of whiskey. My brand was E.G. Booze, that came in a cabin-shaped bottle that said on it: "E.G. Booze, a name so famous it became part of the English language". Then we had another, and another.

Hans suggested we go into the Christmas tree business. He had a big truck in Canada if I would rent a lot to sell them, he'd bring the trees. The first truck load was so fresh it had snow on top of the trees. Hans said he had some farmer buddies who also weren't using their trucks right now, and they could bring more trees. Of course, they brought their families and stayed free in my motel. I opened a second lot and ultimately three more, so I had five Christmas tree lots. Needless to say, I dropped out of college.

The problem in South L.A was, you had to man the lots 24 hours a day or the neighbors would take your trees. But a bigger problem was that this was the first year that the markets sold trees as a loss-leader item.

Before we learned that, it seemed we were going to make a killing. Tom Miller, a college buddy I hired to help me, and I went to the Mercedes dealership to look at the new 300 SLs. We kept waiting for "the big weekend." On Christmas Day we had over a thousand of very fresh trees and had to pay $27 per load at the dump. In 1956, twenty-seven bucks was a lot of money.

That night, a fight occurred outside a kitchen unit on the other side of my motel. I responded and when I tried to break it up, both combatants turned on me and backed me into an alcove. Just then we heard a loud voice say "HOLD IT." When the two turned they were looking down the barrel of Hans' .44 revolver which to me looked big enough to climb into. He marched them out onto Figueroa and told them not to come back.

Before our lease ran out on the money-losing motel, I desperately needed a job to support our family. I answered a two-line ad in the Los Angeles Times.

The company was American Service Bureau, a nationwide "inspection company" that conducted minimal, overt neighborhood investigations of mostly life insurance applicants.

They hired me as an inspector. It was piece work that paid $1.15 for a regular report and $3.45 for a "special narrative report". My territory was South Los Angeles, a mostly African American neighborhood.

Marcia did such a good job typing my reports that they offered me a position as Assistant Manager of their Los Angeles office. In the interview by the branch manager Maynard Hummel, he offered me a salary of $425 per month. Since the best job I had ever had at that point was staff sergeant in the airborne infantry which paid $300 if I jumped out of perfectly good airplanes, I immediately took it. Periodically my salary was raised $20. My first Christmas, a letter arrived from the company president in Chicago containing a $200 check. Nearly a half month's pay.

After six months, they hired an additional guy named Germenkamp to be a second assistant manager. He was about five years older than me and had worked for Retail Credit. The next Christmas the president's letter held a check for only $100. No explanation.

Then the company decided to open a Long Beach branch. I was hopeful since I had six months seniority over Germenkamp. But they gave him the promotion. Now I was doing my job and his, since he transferred to Long Beach. My pay, which by then was up to $500 per month, stayed the same. I was supervising over two dozen inspectors and Germenkamp had about six. My days were very busy. The extra work and no raise and the reduced bonus combined with not getting the Long Beach branch, all began to make me a little disgruntled.

Shortly before Christmas 1959, a vice president arrived from Chicago. His name was Otto Elder. After watching me work for fifteen minutes he informed me that I was doing everything wrong and "this is the way we do it in Chicago." I tried to explain that Los Angeles is considerably different, to no avail. So, I stood up and said, "You know Mr. Elder, you're kind of a dumb sonofabitch." He didn't have enough nerve to fire me himself, but he obviously told Hummel to get rid of me.

When Elder went back to Chicago, Maynard Hummel called me into his office and said he had 23 years invested and had to stick it out for his pension. But since I was young, I should look around for something else. I appreciated his not firing me on the spot. Christmas was the next week, so I went to the L.A. Times again. This led me to begin working for Krout & Schneider in January 1960.

Sixty-two years later, I am still there and now Chairman.

MY FIRST TRIP TO PHOENIX

Currently, I reside in Sun Lakes, Arizona, a southern suburb of Phoenix, but in 1962, I lived in Norwalk, California.

I was the lead field investigator for the Los Angeles office of Krout and Schneider, a detective agency with ten offices covering the West Coast. I did both surveillance and all types of investigation. One of our best clients was Southern Pacific Railway, though we sometimes also worked for Santa Fe and Union Pacific. I mingled with all those guys at the annual railroad golf tournament.

Our manager got a call from Southern Pacific requesting we send an experienced operative to Phoenix. They explained that because of the confidential nature of the job, they didn't want to trust the assignment to an Arizona agency. So, I headed to the Los Angeles International Airport. I wasn't very impressed with the Sky Harbor Airport in Phoenix which was about the size of the bus depot in Los Angeles. I rented a car and got started.

The case involved a law suit by a guy I'll call Duckett who was a Justice of the Peace in Arizona. Duckett was drunk as a skunk one night and drove his car into the side of a stopped Southern Pacific train at a crossing in the boon docks. He sued the railroad for having the temerity to have their train in his way.

The case wouldn't have worried SP once they had the drunk driving conviction to show his condition, but Duckett, using his judicial office, was able to get his traffic case continued, repeatedly. The railroad had little evidence to present at his substantial trial for damages against the railroad and the date for his trial against the railroad was rapidly approaching.

Somehow, SP had the name of a Maricopa County deputy who had been at the accident scene when Duckett ran into the side of the stopped train. I contacted him and met him at the dinky Maricopa Court House which also held the Sheriff's office. I told him the Sheriff's record's people weren't cooperating with my request regarding pulling the citation. He asked me to meet him there at 5:15 PM.

He was in uniform and using a master key, he unlocked the door of the records room and led me to several file cabinets where traffic citations were filed in drawers chronologically. In 1962, the system was quite primitive. But amazingly, we found the carbon copy of the citation. He informed me that under Arizona law, DUI's had to be certified by a chemist whose report of alcoholic blood content is normally stapled to the copy of the citation. The chemist's report was missing but there were two staple holes in the citation. We suspected Duckett had been able to tamper with the records. The deputy gave me a signed statement attesting to the usual procedures and what we had found.

The deputy gave me the name of the chemist who would have administered the blood test. When I tried to contact the chemist, I found he was in the hospital with terminal cancer. I interviewed him at his hospital bedside. He clearly remembered the case because of Duckett being who he was. He even remembered the high number for Duckett's blood test and gave me a signed statement that proved Duckett was extremely drunk when he ran into the side of the train. This wrapped up my investigation, so I headed for the airport.

I was on a three-lane street some distance from the airport and approaching a railroad crossing whose red lights were flashing. I was the second car from the tracks and there was a black and white Phoenix PD patrol car directly behind me. I heard the loud whistle of the approaching train which didn't let up and sounded urgent. From my position, I couldn't see what the reason for the unrelenting horn was about. But there was suddenly a crash and I got a brief glimpse of a vehicle being struck and catapulted down the tracks by the Union Pacific freight train which must have been still going 40 mph at impact, even with the brakes.

The black and white pulled to the right and the officer jumped out, so I did the same. He and I ran down the side of the train eventually getting to a severely damaged red pick-up truck. The officer and I looked inside and saw no one so we started to search the right of way. That was when we heard a voice say, "Are you guys looking for me?"

The pick-up driver related how he had just bought the truck that day and barely got out when it stalled on the track. I ran back to my rental car and retrieved my statement pad. The train crew was gathering and were all pretty shook up but relieved to find they hadn't killed somebody.

I got signed statements from everybody even including the cop and the pick-up driver. Once the UP got the train past the crossing, I was able to get on my way to the airport. At my office I sent the statements to the Union Pacific Claims Manager gratis.

Investigating one train wreck but reporting on a second left a vivid memory of my first trip to Phoenix. Oh, and I forgot to mention, it was on this trip I saw my first Road Runner.

THE STOGIE FROM SKOKIE

Sears in Los Angeles had been my client for many years. Their claims manager was a lovely spinster lady named Clara. Unfortunately, I lost that account in 1968 when I had to refuse to do a rope job on one of their claimants. The plaintiff's bar had put the kibosh on roping that year by claiming that investigators were "agents" of lawyers and therefore prohibited from contacting a represented claimant.

Clara was forced to hire a different investigative firm which ultimately resulted in bad law and an infamous decision known as *Noble vs Sears* that is the bane of investigations even today. But that's another story.

The Sears home office was in Skokie, Illinois, and someone, (possibly Clara) recommended our firm, to do a heavy-duty investigation. I'll call the subject Mr. Stogie, since he was seldom seen without a big cigar in his mouth. He was the primary buyer for a substantial portion of what Sears imported from China and other countries in that part of the world. A very important job.

Skokie told me they suspected Mr. Stogie was on the take, receiving kickbacks big time and as a result he was suspected of being a high roller in Las Vegas. They made it clear that cost was not an issue. They needed results. They had information that he was due back in the States on a flight from the Orient that was due into San Francisco. They wanted him under surveillance and suspected he might head for Las Vegas.

Since it was a one-shot deal, I took no chances. Operatives Jim Morey and Basilio Villanueva were sent by car to Vegas. I flew to San Francisco and was joined by Skip Andreasen from our San Francisco office. Sure as hell, Mr. Stogie landed in SF and had a big cigar in his mouth the first time I saw him. He checked in at the counter for a Vegas flight and I was able to get a seat on the same flight, so I sent Skip home and alerted Morey and Villanueva what flight to meet in Vegas.

Villanueva met the plane and Morey stayed in the car. Villanueva and I followed Mr. Stogie to the luggage area. A little quicker than we hoped, the sky cap grabbed Mr. Stogie's luggage and put it in a cab. Although Morey was ready for action, he barely picked up Villanueva and me before the cab took off to beat hell, destination unknown. The light was red as we reached the intersection. I told Morey to bust the signal, though I think he would have anyway. The screeching and horn blowing was substantial, but Morey avoided an accident and stayed with the cab. If we had lost him here, the case would have been over, since we had no idea which hotel he was going to.

At the Riviera Hotel Mr. Stogie climbed out of the cab and headed for the check-in counter. As he approached the counter, one of the clerks shouted out a welcome greeting to him and tossed him a key from five feet away. He was obviously a regular. He headed for the Tower elevator.

I told Morey to get us a room with two beds figuring to take shifts. He came back shortly to advise that since it was Memorial Day weekend, there were no rooms.

I approached the counter picking a bald-headed clerk like myself. Putting a double sawbuck in my hand barely showing a corner of the bill, I said I had no reservation but needed a room. These were the days when twenty bucks was a lot of money. The clerk grinned knowingly and said all he had was a suite in the Tower but he would give it to me for the regular room rate as he palmed the bill. The suite was huge and nice. Two bedrooms, two baths, living room/dining with a huge wet bar.

After about an hour, Mr. Stogie exited the Tower elevator, crossed the casino and said hello to a middle-aged woman at the black jack table. Mrs. Stogie had preceded him. These were the days when the hotel paged guests by name on the casino floor. We set up a system using the name Houston Antoine for paging.

Mr. Stogie was a high stakes gambler who both shot craps and played poker. His wife, on the other hand, stuck with black jack. I followed her to the cashier and observed her to ask for and open her safe deposit box. Therein appeared to be sizable stacks of $100 bills and some jewelry. After watching them both for three days, and noting Mrs. Stogie only went to her safe deposit when Mr. Stogie was up in their room, I think he may have been unaware of the contents of her safe deposit box.

After giving the Illinois Sears headquarters a verbal, they said they had enough. I'm sure Mr. Stogie didn't survive the rest of the investigation into his kickbacks.

GOOD SAMARITAN HOSPITAL

When I began employment at Krout and Schneider in Los Angeles in 1960, it had offices in ten cities covering the West Coast.

Shortly after my employment we received an undercover assignment at Good Samaritan Hospital. They were having shortages of sheets and blankets. They wished to put an operative in the laundry. The pay for their laundry workers was $1.33 per hour. Fortunately, Krout and Schneider paid me an hourly bonus above my Good Samaritan pay check.

Knowing I was going to need work boots, I went out and purchased some leather, ankle high boots that looked great. Working in the laundry, the leather got soaked through the first day and my boots were wet the entire 30 days I worked there. In that month, I got promoted three times from extractor man, to assistant wash man, to wash man.

The workers in the laundry were all Hispanic and seemed a little suspicious of what a gringo was doing there. The only thing that helped my acceptance were the tattoos on my forearms. But I had to be careful of how I spoke and got sharp looks if I used a word of any substance. The manager and his assistant were gringos, mean and unfriendly.

The soiled laundry came down chutes that emptied above the giant washing machines. When the stainless-steel door on top of the washer was opened, you pulled a rope and the soiled laundry tumbled out to be jammed into each side of the washer. Some laundry was dirtier than others. The babies in the nursery were indiscriminate.

Surgery laundry was surprising. Believe it or not, they laundered and reused sponges which had to be laundered in a small machine. Each load of sponges had to be rinsed several times in cold water until the red color of the drain water turned clear, then they used the hot. I wasn't involved in the drying and sanitizing, but I know they were careful.

We had to be very cautious pushing the contents from surgery into the washers because they often included surgical instruments and an occasional hypodermic needle which would stick your hand or arm.

When the wash cycle was complete the extractor man had to bring two half clam shell stainless steel perforated tubs on the overhead hydraulic hook and place each half against the side of the wash tub. Then the contents of the washers are emptied into the half-circled tubs.

Once each half circle tub was full, they were rolled together to make a circle. Then I brought the overhead hydraulic hook to hoist the tubs and pushed them along the track before lowering them into the circular centrifuge extractor which is about five feet in diameter. The whirling extractor shook the building, kind of like your washer at home when a load gets unbalanced. Once the load has had the bulk of the water removed, the damp laundry went to the huge dryers.

During the washing laundry cycles, I had no opportunity to observe any theft. But on my lunch hour in the parking lot I saw the manager and his assistant loading sheets and blankets into their cars on several occasions. Since they were doing this in broad daylight, I wondered if somehow what they were doing was authorized. But when this was reported to the nuns who run the hospital, they followed up and confirmed it was unauthorized and this explained the constant shrinkage.

We received a nice congratulatory letter at our office from the sisters for my personnel file. My boots finally got dried out.

Being on my feet on concrete eight hours per day with no opportunity to rest reminded me that manual labor in factory-like settings doing undercover investigation was not for me, although I do feel a kinship with Good Samaritan Hospital.

HOWARD HUGHES AND ME

I began working for Krout & Schneider in 1960. Our office received a TWA subpoena in 1961 to be served on Howard Hughes and I was assigned to serve it.

I knew very little about the man, who was famous, but not like he is now, so I went to the Hollywood Library and began my research. Hughes headquarters was a building at 7000 Romaine in Hollywood. The word was that he maintained a bungalow at the Beverly Hills Hotel with wife, actress Jean Peters.

Marcia and I rented a bungalow in the rear of the hotel. I knew better than to press the bell staff for information. But I observed one bungalow that constantly had various people seated on the porch and when some of the regulars were not there, a bellman would take the seat. In view of Hughes fabulous disinformation system, he probably wasn't there. According to my assignment, I was on the lookout for a guy in shabby Mexican sandals driving an old Chevy.

During the period when I was looking for Hughes, Walter Winchell reported seeing Mr. and Mrs. Hughes at a night club in Mexico City. The same day, gossip columnist Louella Parsons reported seeing the couple at Ciro's on the Sunset

Strip. I'm sure neither was true. I never served him, and neither has anyone else.

When he needed to meet with someone, he would fly his DC-3 into Cloverfield in Santa Monica. After his staff cleared the visitor, Hughes would land, pick up the visitor, fly around and land to drop him off after the meeting.

Las Vegas population was 80,000 in 1960. In 1966 everything changed when Howard Hughes decided to occupy the top floor of the Desert Inn. After a couple of months, the hotel decided to evict Hughes to make room for high-rollers. So, he bought the Hotel. And then he bought some more. Hughes is a major reason today's population of greater Las Vegas is over two million.

"In 1960, Hughes was ultimately forced out of management of TWA, although he continued to own 78% of the company. In 1961, TWA filed suit against Hughes Tool Company, claiming that the latter had violated antitrust law by using TWA as a captive market for aircraft trading. The claim was largely dependent upon obtaining testimony from Hughes himself. Hughes went into hiding and refused to testify. A default judgment was issued against Hughes Tool Company for $135 million in 1963, but was overturned by the Supreme Court of the United States in 1973, on the basis that Hughes was immune from prosecution. In 1966, Hughes was forced to sell his TWA shares. The sale of his TWA shares brought Hughes $546,549,771." *Wikipedia*®

MURDER HE WROTE

Although I have been a private investigator for over 65 years, I have only worked seven murder investigations. This is one of the most interesting.

We received an assignment from a downtown Los Angeles law firm representing a business woman in Belgium. She wanted to prove that her late husband, Arnie Tali, had not committed a Beverly Hills murder. She was apparently in civil litigation with the husband of one of the murder victims, Lloyd Cotsen, president of Neutrogena company.

In 1979, a ski masked intruder entered the Cotsen's home on Bedford Drive, confronted Mrs. Cotsen, probably rendered her incapacitated with chloroform, then tied her up and gagged her. He is suspected to have been waiting for Mr. Cotsen to return home from a business trip to New York.

About three hours later, Mrs. Cotsen's 14-year-old son Noah arrived home from school. He was also tied and gagged. Shortly thereafter, a school friend of Noah's arrived and he was also tied and gagged.

An hour or more later, a couple who rented a small cottage in the rear of the Cotsen estate arrived in the backyard to retrieve their mail and also entered the home. They were also tied up, but not very well. The male was able to free his hands and escaped out the front door shouting to the female he was going for help. The female freed herself too and ran towards the back door. The intruder fired a .22 caliber pistol equipped with a silencer at her four times, but missed.

The intruder panicked, re-entered the living room, and shot Mrs. Cotsen and each boy once in the head, killing them. He then stole one of the Cotsen's cars and drove two blocks to where he probably had his own rental car parked on the street. He apparently threw some Mexican ammunition down a storm drain, and departed. The ammunition was later discovered by the Beverly Hills police.

BACKGROUND

Mrs. Joanne Cotsen was the daughter of Emanuel Stolaroff who owned a small company named Natone that made and sold cosmetics to the film industry. Lloyd Cotsen had graduated from Princeton and obtained an MBA degree from Harvard. After marrying Joanne Stolaroff, Cotsen went to work for Mr. Stolaroff and became interested in the soap and cosmetics business.

A man named Edmund Fromont in Belgium had invented a shampoo and soap product he named Neutrogena. Stolaroff and Cotsen arranged to purchase a license from Fromont to make and distribute Neutrogena in the United States. Cotsen changed the name of Stolaroff's company from Natone to Neutrogena and the American and non-Belgian business expanded rapidly under Cotsen's leadership.

When Fromont died, he left his Belgian Neutrogena company to his mistress, Marianne. She then married a Belgian man named Arnie Tali. He started running the Belgian wing of the Neutrogena named company.

Lloyd Cotsen contacted Arnie Tali and repeatedly offered to purchase licensing to sell Neutrogena products in other parts of the world in addition to the U.S., but was turned down by Tali. According to witnesses, Arnie Tali developed a hatred for Lloyd Cotsen.

As the Beverly Hills Police continued the investigation of the Cotsen murders, trying to pin down a suspect in October 1979, another notorious crime occurred at that time which got their attention due to its ghastly nature and similar characteristics involving Mexican manufactured ammunition.

The Bonaventure Hotel case involved the Israeli murder of a couple in downtown Los Angeles, arising from a dope deal gone bad. Cotsen's file at the Beverly Hills Police contained notes about the Bonaventure murders, so they were looking at them at the same time and some journalists were speculating about a possible connection.

To summarize: Israeli dope dealers had a falling out in Los Angeles so the Israeli enforcer for the gang rented a room for a meeting at the Bonaventure Hotel. When a couple who were the California wing of the dope gang responsible for sales in the Los Angeles area entered the hotel room, the Israeli hit man immediately shot them both with a .22 caliber pistol.

He then raped the wounded woman before killing and dismembering her, then dismembered the man. The body parts were placed in suitcases for disposal. These enforcers were ultimately apprehended and incarcerated.

During the same time frame Beverly Hills police discovered airfare and car rental receipts by Arnie Tali showing that he was in Los Angeles at the time the Cotsen murders. They also determined that the chloroform bottle left at the crime scene had come from Belgium and that chloroform was an ingredient of Neutrogena soap.

Beverly Hills PD decided they should interview Arnie Tali and two detectives flew to Belgium. They made an appointment to meet with Tali, but were put off until the next day.

When the detectives arrived the following day, they were informed there had been an "emergency in the night" and Mr. Tali was deceased. He had committed suicide.

Beverly Hills Police made the assumption that Tali had committed the Cotsen murders and closed their file.

Based on the evidence contained in the police files, I reported to my client that the evidence of Tali's guilt appeared very strong and that, in my opinion, it would not be possible to prove Arnie Tali didn't do it.

According to news articles, Lloyd Cotsen sold Neutrogena in 1994 for approximately $350 million to Johnson & Johnson.

FISHING WITH THE FEDS

or

The Case of the Lying Banker

The boss's daughter was a Jewish princess from San Francisco. A cute one too. Popular in college, she married a doctor who gave her two kids and a divorce. Needless to say, her Dad was dismayed. But Sam loved those little girls so much, he never spoke of his disappointment.

There was good news around the bend. After a respite, Prince Charming arrived looking more promising than the doctor. They married and moved to the East Coast. Prince was a handsome, suave, Scandinavian who allegedly spoke seven languages and oozed class and charm. When you introduced him to your lady, you could almost feel his hand in her panties. He was bold and smart and I liked him.

Prince was a fish broker from New Jersey. We're talking quantity here. Million-dollar lines of credit, wheeling and dealing all over the world in shrimp and lobster. Highly perishable, risky, and profitable, if done right. He frequently traveled to South America and Europe. The boss was delighted that the Princess and his granddaughters had at last found happiness after the pain of the divorce. So delighted, I later learned, that Sam backed Prince's action with a substantial amount of investment.

I was the new manager in Los Angeles. I had never met Prince and didn't know about the boss's daughter, but I sure knew who the boss was. Sam called to say I would be getting a call from Prince about a rip-off, and that I should give it special attention and maybe a little discount on the bill. Sam never worked for free. Not even for his brothers little Charlie and Maurice the Hat. But that's another story.

Soon Prince called with the poop from New Jersey. Some new customers in Los Angeles whose names were Wilson and Jones, had ordered one hundred grand's worth of lobster to be shipped to a bona fide warehouse in the packinghouse district. Prince's bank verified adequate balances with their bank. This was backed by a claimed substantial line of credit and a five-year business history with their bank.

Prince had never heard of Wilson and Jones, but it was an important order at a good price and he put it on the plane. Deals have to be made fast and depend on airfreight to deliver the next day. This necessary urgency increases the financial risk. Three days later, when it was time for the bank to transfer funds, there was only peanuts in the Wilson and Jones account. Their bank denied verifying their account. The warehouse said the goods were moved out the same day they arrived. Prince was in big trouble and kicking himself for not double checking with his Los Angeles contacts on who these guys were.

I had worked around the packinghouses and was somewhat familiar with the ethnic nature of the food business. Shrimp and lobster are more esoteric because they are so perishable, but the genre of the players in the business is the same. Damon Runyon would've had a field day. I found out which trucker signed for the tails at the warehouse. From the trucking company I learned they delivered the lobster to five different legitimate wholesalers in the Vernon area of Los Angeles.

At each wholesaler, the attitude and story, was the same:

"Yeah, Wilson and Jones offered them a good deal at below market. Maybe the price seemed too good to be true, but the merchandise was good and came from a reputable broker in New Jersey. No, they didn't think to call Prince even though they had never heard of Wilson and Jones before. (This in a business where everybody knows everybody.) No, they don't have the lobster anymore. They sold it immediately. They did nothing wrong."

We would have a fat chance of recovering from these guys. A prosecution for receiving stolen goods was next to impossible. After all, did you ever see a lobster with a serial number? Besides, however satisfying and noble, prosecution seldom puts money back in the client's pocket.

Bottom line: My client had jumped at the chance to sell a big order for a top price without haggling. The wholesalers jumped at the chance to buy good lobster at below market with no questions asked even though they should have suspected it was hot. So, what's new? Greed over-rides common sense once again.

I had a good description of the con men. Flashy dressers, big cigars. A brand new Coupe de ville with Vogue tires. The epitome of class before the Mercedes/BMW days. One wholesaler who went to lunch with them remembered the license plate frame from the big Cadillac dealer in Downey, a Southeast Los Angeles suburb. The branch of Insecurity Bank which verified the balances and credit line to Prince's bank was also located in Downey.

At Insecurity bank I asked to see Evans who Prince's bank said had verified the account of Wilson and Jones. Evans was the number three man in the branch, a loan officer who handled mostly car deals. He was trying to appear cooperative but he was nervous. He admitted that the bank only had a relationship with Wilson and Jones for 90 days. They opened an account with $25,000 and told him they would soon transfer substantially more funds as they were going to start doing business in a big way in the Downey/Los Angeles area.

The $100,000 worth of checks from the five wholesalers were deposited over a two-day period. There was now less than 100 bucks in the account. No, he had not verified a six-figure balance or a line of credit to the New Jersey bank. Sorry, he couldn't help me further.

The address of the residence the bank had for Wilson and Jones, was a mail drop. The lobster were gone. Wilson and Jones were gone. Nobody admitted doing anything wrong.

What proof did we have if they did. Wilson and Jones had once again worked a classic scam counting on human nature.

The young bank officer has a new house in the suburbs, a new car, a couple of kids and was strung out with payments, hoping for a promotion at the bank. The big new commercial account would be a feather in his cap. Evans was flattered when Wilson and Jones took him to lunches and dinners at the best eateries.

Wanting to help his new friends Evans had prevailed on the Downey Cadillac dealer to sell a Coupe de ville to Jones with a minimum down in spite of the lack of specifics on their out-of-state credit. In those days, credit had to be verified by mail or phone, and Wilson and Jones had given the bank two numbers to call in the East who gave them glowing references. Ordinarily they pay cash they said, but a substantial amount of their funds was in transit, from the sale of their operation out-of-state.

They had in fact deposited 25 big ones at Insecurity's Downey branch. Evans assured the dealer they were going to be doing a lot of business in the area and would be a good source of future business. The Cadillac dealer often needed the bankers help and he relied on the banker's financial expertise. He was happy to make the sale, particularly when they didn't quibble on the price for a car loaded with extras including the Vogue tires. Greed strikes again.

I was pretty sure locating and arresting Wilson and Jones would not get my client's money back quickly, if at all. On the other hand, Insecurity bank was a viable donkey to pin the tail on, even though they too were victims. Falsely ver-ifying the account for five years and a higher balance was a no-no which carried some civil liability. But I needed to put some pressure on them to admit it. I did not know if Evans was in on the theft, or if he too had been duped.

I returned to the bank and met with the branch manager/vice president. He left his office to talk to Evans, then came back and stonewalled me. My client's Los Angeles lawyers called the bank's lawyers. No Mea Culpa they said. I reluc-tantly put a stakeout on the mail drop. This was expensive and sometimes people don't come by for a week. The boss would not be pleased.

Then Maria, my investigative supervisor, reminded me to turn my brain on. She had reviewed the file and found Jones driver's license records showed the phony mail drop address alright, but he had an accident with a rental car three months before in Huntington Park. She did some more digging and produced an accident report showing the accident location to be on a residential street. Jones had been backing out of the driveway and clipped a car driving by.

Following that lead, Maria sent an operative to the accident site for a look-see. Guess what? There, parked in the drive-way in the middle of the block was a shiny new Coupe de ville with Vogue tires and the license number we were look-ing for. I instructed my people to make no contacts and stay on the car. We pulled off the mail drop. Now we had a sure thing.

Knowing how much enthusiasm the FBI usually has for dealing with private investigators, I asked my client's lawyer to make the call and file a complaint. The next morning, two agents showed up at my office. Saving the best for last I laid it out for them and gave them copies of our investigative reports. The surveillance reports hadn't been completed yet and they were surprised when I told them I currently had Wilson and Jones under surveillance.

FBI guys love to make arrests. They take squads of people and usually the local cops, who hate them because they treat them like poor relatives. They said they would scoop up Wilson and Jones but I didn't go with them to see the fun. I had more important things to do and fast.

Busting the rover boys wasn't likely to put the money in my client's pocket. But we were sure as hell going to turn up the heat at the bank. As I drove to the bank, my two-way radio crackled with a message from the operative on the stakeout. The FBI had arrested Wilson and Jones.

At the bank they said Evans was off sick. I set the outdoor speed record driving to Evans home. He greeted me with apprehension. He reluctantly let me in. He asked if I could see him alone and we went into the kitchen. I exaggerated the facts a little and told him the feds had picked up Wilson and Jones who were claiming he was in on it.

I hate this part of the job. I always feel so sorry for the poor, dumb, s.o.b. He looked like he was going to cry. He denied being a co-conspirator, but spilled his guts on having verified the account and credit line. He said Wilson and Jones convinced him they were legitimate businessmen with ample resources. They said there was a hiccup getting a quarter million in balances transferred to his bank. Could he help them out in closing this big important deal by telling the New Jersey bank that they already had the funds in his branch and had been doing business there for five years?

When they deposited the five checks from the wholesalers totaling $100,000, he was sure he had done the right thing and now had secured a first-class client for the bank. Even when they came in the next day to buy the $125,000 cashier's-check he never suspected what was happening. They told him another deal presented itself and they would replenish the account in three days, with even more money.

He gave me a three-page signed statement. That's what I needed to establish the civil liability of the bank. I believed him when he said he had been taken in on the hope of getting a Goldstar. Instead, he got fired.

The FBI drove up as I was getting in my car. I gave them a grin and a wave. They almost took out after me but probably thought it was undignified. The reason the coppers hate the feds is because the FBI agents usually want you to give them everything you have, then say they are sorry but their file is confidential. It comes back to haunt them when everyone else makes it difficult. There <u>are</u> some good agents. My apologies to my ex-agent friends. But it was nice to use them for a change. I never met Wilson or Jones but they did quite a stretch in the federal pen.

When my client's lawyer waved the statement under the bank's nose, their lawyers said to pay. Prince was ecstatic. Sam was proud. I was the fair-haired boy.

A year or so later, Prince came to town and rented a big suite at the Century Plaza. We had drinks there with his lawyer, a local food magnate who had helped on the case, my boss Sam and all our wives. Most of the evening was spent saying what a great guy I was. I loved it.

He took us to dinner at the Beverly Wilshire. Hernando Courtright himself came by the table to ask if everything was all right. He must've been kidding. Prince could sure put on the dog. I really admired him, but I was always uncomfortable with the way he looked at my wife.

THE SPYING SCIENTIST CONSPIRACY

The call came from the Security Director. A giant division of a Fortune 100 company, whose name is a household word, seemed to have a leak in its bidding system. A competitor not only was undercutting their bids on government contracts by fractions, but also seemed to have proprietary product information.

A former sales manager for the division was known to have gone to work for a competitor as a Vice President, but our client had no other possible leads. Our security chief client says that a top scientist and two division managers have recently left the company.

We put the two ex-managers under surveillance and find them meeting with another scientist who is still employed by our client.

Checking corporate filings, we find that the mole employee scientist is listed as an owner in public records of the new competitive company.

Surveillance of the former employee drew a blank for a week until we tailed him to a fancy restaurant with valet parking. Here he met with three other men whom we videotaped leaving the lunch spot. As their cars were delivered, we zoomed in on the license plates.

Our client easily recognized two current employees on the tape. One was a scientist involved in product development and the other mole, a key production manager. The vehicle registrations provided the name of the third man, a key exec at the competitor.

A specialist was recruited to work undercover in the scientist's department and our client fed the mole scientist disinformation on bids and specs for several weeks. We continued to gather evidence and document meetings.

When maximum evidence had been developed, our client's lawyers made their move. A civil suit for injunctive relief for theft of trade secrets, and unfair competition stopped the thieves in their tracks.

Faced with heavy civil liability and potential criminal charges, the new company flounders and they are all looking for work elsewhere.

Another industrial espionage scheme had bitten the dust.

DENIM Part one

The storied Levi Strauss came from Bavaria to San Francisco in 1853 and sold dry goods. Eventually he partnered with a Nevada tailor who initially bought canvas fabric from him, to produce canvas pants for workers. The myth that they began making these pants for miners in the 1849 Gold Rush may not be true since they didn't start making the Levi pants until about 1870.

Strauss never married and had no children of his own. He lived with his brother-in-law David Stern and family and when he died, he left his 55% of Levi Strauss Co. to his four nephews. Nephew Jacob Stern took over as President and the business grew but had periodic set-backs.

In 1914, Walter Haas Sr., son of the founder of Hellman Haas Grocery Company (later to become Smart and Final) married Elise Stern, granddaughter of David Stern and grand-niece of Levi Strauss. After serving in WWI, Haas returned home in 1919 and started working for Levi Strauss Co. rising to CEO. Walter Haas Sr. is one of San Francisco's most famous and influential philanthropists. He is credited with saving the Levi Strauss operation and making it into the success it is today.

Walter Haas Sr. had a sister named Ruth Lilienthal. She was never involved in the operation of the company, but she enjoyed the perks of being a minor shareholder and member of the prestigious family. Some said she was essentially a playgirl who never worked a day in her life.

Levi Strauss was a private company until the need for more capital would lead to taking the company public in 1971. One of the loose ends was a fund they had created similar to modern ESOPs (Employee Stock Ownership Programs). This fund issued stock to key employees and when they left the firm, bought it back. In some fashion, over the years, Ruth Lilienthal had accumulated some stock through this fund.

In preparation for the IPO, Walter Haas Jr. and his brother Peter who were now running the firm, wanted to buy out small shareholders to make the public offering a smooth deal. Among other purchases, the brothers acquired Ruth Lilienthal's shares prior to announcing the IPO. When the public offering was announced, Levi Strauss shares increased in value substantially. Ruth died January 7, 1975.

While Ruth Lilienthal had not taken any legal action during her life, her heirs no doubt were convinced she had been screwed by her brother's sons. So, they hired my friend, attorney Richard Oshman, to sue them. To do this, Oshman, a Jew himself, and less than famous legal practitioner in Los Angeles, had to go to court in San Francisco against not only the leading Jewish family, but the most highly regarded philanthropic family in the City.

As Oshman's investigator, my job was to find an insider or former insider who would attest to the Haas brother's intention to buy Ruth's shares for less than they would be worth after going public.

I went to San Francisco and its environs and interviewed a number of former Levi executives. Some were actually friendly, but none wanted to be the smoking gun. Still, the best evidence on the face of it, were the dates of the transactions. Just a week or two between the purchase and the announcement.

In court in San Francisco, Oshman was treated like an ambulance chaser from of all places, *"Los Angeles"! EGADS!* Oshman was treated with disdain but was able to drive a nuisance settlement of about $3,000,000. His one million dollar-plus fee was more money than he ever dreamed of in the little firm of Oshman, Brownfield, and Smith.

Regrettably, my friend didn't live happily ever after. He put the million smackers in a tax shelter the IRS claimed was not lawful. They chased him for years after he died from leukemia as well as his widow. My wife Marcia who had the same, somewhat rare blood type, gave Dick two direct blood transfusions before he passed. He was a good friend.

DENIM Part two

A lawyer client and friend, Drew McConnell whose father was once State Insurance Commissioner, sponsored me to join Wilshire Country Club. For the first year I wore long sleeved shirts to hide my tattoos before I noticed a couple of other members had tattoos, albeit smaller than mine

There were three other members, one a former admiral, who couldn't pass me without glancing at my tattoos. But for the most part, I was accepted.

Caddies were required at Wilshire and because of that requirement, we had an excellent caddie staff most of whom lived up the street in an older hotel. The tee markers on each hole are steel oil drilling bits which were donated by Howard Hughes in memory of his father who invented the two con roller bits.

On my first day, they initiated me by putting me with "Al the Caddie." He was the oldest caddie and served as the historian. When we reached the 8th Green, near the 9th Tee, Al pointed to the classic two-story Spanish style mansion next to the green.

Al related how one morning as his foursome was putting out on hole #8, actress Jean Harlow stepped out on the balcony of Howard Hughes abode without benefit of clothing. According to Al, Miss Harlow looked down at the speechless golfers and bade them "Good Morning" as if this was normal. Following the pleasantries, she remained standing there nude for a period before returning inside. Al said there weren't any birdies that morning.

So how does this relate to Denim? The Marciano brothers bought that former Howard Hughes mansion at 211 S. Muirfield in Hancock Park and owned it for many years.

One day, one of my lawyer clients asked me to accompany him to GUESS headquarters in downtown Los Angeles. By then the Marciano's were somewhat famous, but their utilitarian offices at the factory were not at all ostentatious. I met with Paul and Georges Marciano concerning a theft problem.

Like many garment factories, GUESS had to be on guard against jeans being sold out the back door of the factory for cash. But that's another story. So many years after my first experience with denim and Levi Strauss, I was still involved with denim.

Interestingly, I had another case involving the home next door that also backed up to Wilshire Country Club. This is a nice neighborhood. So even though the fabric Denim and the Marcianos had nothing to do with the home next door, I still associate the former Howard Hughes mansion with the next-door home of Henry T. Mudd. Mr. Mudd was the namesake of prestigious Harvey Mudd University and President of Pacific Mutual Life Insurance Company as well as Cyprus Mines.

I received a call from the #3 biggest law firm in LA asking that we initiate surveillance of Mr. Mudd, a tall, white-haired, Patrician looking gentleman who drove a Bentley.

To our surprise, Mr. Mudd had a habit of trolling for hookers on Sunset Boulevard in his Bentley. Later, we learned he paid the rent for an apartment in WeHo, (West Hollywood) that was inhabited by ladies of questionable repute. Repeated evening surveillances revealed he consistently drove up and down Sunset, picking up interesting companions. After ten days, we were asked to discontinue.

I received a call from Mrs. Mudd asking that I be present on the next evening when she would be meeting with Mr. Mudd. I asked if there were firearms in the house and when she responded yes, I arranged to come by the house and pick them up. She had a picnic basket full of hand guns including a Mauser machine pistol which I put in an associate's vehicle.

On the next evening, my operative, John Eppick, stayed in the kitchen with the cook and butler who was serving their dinner in the master suite. I was shown into the library where I remained for about an hour. At the end of that time Mrs. Mudd said all was well and I could leave.

Mr. Mudd died of leukemia in 1990. Following Mr. Mudd's death, there ensued multiple litigations involving seven women who claimed to be his mistresses. Marvin Mitchelson, the lawyer famous for initiating palimony suits, was heavily involved. It was revealed that Mr. Mudd had lavished considerable funds on these women including purchasing homes for them and paying one a monthly allowance of $8,600. I can't make this stuff up.

MY FIRST SAILING VOYAGE

It's true that I was born in Los Angeles, but raised on a farm in Canada. LA was on the water, while we had little in Alberta, unless you count summer trips for a swim in the Old Man River, near Monarch. But my sailing story really begins in 1941.

My family liked to winter in California until I was school age, then the trips South were less frequent. In the third grade and the seventh grade, I transferred to an LA school for three months or so when my parents longed for California.

On December 7, 1941, three days after my eighth birthday, I had a quarter burning a hole in my pocket. I walked to the Nuway Chili Dog stand at Pico Blvd and Bundy Drive from my Aunt Virginia's house on Barrington. The late Herbert Chance, the owner operator, had perfected a way of preparing the meat for the chili which was never equaled. Hot dogs elsewhere were ten cents, but Chance got 25 cents for a delicious, superior product. I'll never forget that day. At Aunt Ginner's, I later heard the Japanese had bombed Pearl Harbor.

Fast forward to 1964. I'm now a private investigator mingling with other PI's. One was George Gibbs, fourteen years my senior but also born in December. Both Sagittarians.

George was raised in Porterville up in the San Joaquin and got into the patrol business when he won a one-car operation from a guy in a poker game when he was going to UCLA. George built up a substantial West Los Angeles residential patrol business and dabbled in investigation as well. He had a gaggle of repeat clients in the Brentwood area who frequently tasked him with domestic stuff that was often pretty silly. I helped him one night with a Brentwood body guard assignment, but that's another story.

As the years went by George and I discovered a mutual craving for chili dogs from the Nuway, so we often met there. We became best friends. We were both founding members of the California Association of Licensed Investigators CALI.

George Gibbs served as President of CALI in 1971/1972. I occupied the position as President in 1977/1978, although I had earlier been Chairman of the Board in 1972. At the time, CALI had 1900 members across the State

One day in 1974, George said, "We ought to buy a boat." So, we started to look for one. When the yacht salesman would ask us what kind of boat we were looking for, George always replied, "One with four windows," which puzzled the salesman. Although neither of us had ever sailed, we decided that we wanted a sail boat. We found a two-year old 30' Islander that had been repossessed by the bank. It was a beautiful sloop except for the life size painting of an Indian, peering into the distance on the transom with the name, "*Fuckawi*."

The boat was in drydock in the Marina at Alamitos Bay, next to Long Beach. Once we finalized the purchase, I started spending weekends scrubbing the name and the Indian's image off the fiberglass. We christened her the "*Sagittarius*".

Since George and I and the Nuway were West Los Angeles oriented, we needed a closer spot to berth her, not Long Beach. The owners of my long-time downtown club, the Los Angeles Athletic Club, the Hathaways, also owned Riviera Country Club and the California Yacht Club, in Marina Del Rey. So, I joined CYC and they assigned me a slip directly in front of Charlie Brown's bay-side restaurant, a premium location.

The day to take delivery of the *Sagittarius* arrived so George and I met the yacht salesman who represented the bank, at Alamitos Bay. We anticipated a long day around the Palos Verdes peninsula to Marina Del Rey, but we underestimated.

The salesman was in a hurry to get rid of us and was stupefied when we told him neither of us had ever sailed before. He reluctantly agreed to give us a lesson which consisted of two rounds of the Bay and his best wishes 20 minutes later.

George agreed that we should gas up before we started so we fully filled the fuel tank while running the exhaust fan. We motored towards the breakwater and once we had passed it, raised the mainsail like the salesman had shown us. We had not charted a course but relied on dead reckoning to get us past Palos Verde. Alas, every time we thought we had tacked sufficiently to get around the tip of the peninsula, we didn't have room to get by so we tacked further out to sea several times.

When I went below after a while, I smelled the strong odor of gasoline. Lifting the cover from the bilge, I determined that the odor emanated from below, and that we had gasoline in the bilge. A shocking development. Unbeknownst to us, we later found out someone had loosened a hose clamp on the fuel filler pipe so that every time we tacked, and the boat keeled over, the full fuel tank dripped fuel into the bilge.

Finally rounding Palos Verdes, it was all up hill to Marina Del Rey. We needed to use the auxiliary motor. But we feared that starting the motor could ignite the fuel fumes in the bilge, even though we had pumped it. We waited until we were near another boat before I started the motor, in case we needed post-explosion rescue. We didn't blow up.

We finally passed Redondo Beach as it grew later and the sun tired of shining. Dead reckoning continued. The time it had taken us to tack around Palos Verdes was much longer than we had anticipated. Several hours longer.

Finally, it looked like we were approaching the jetty into Marina Del Rey, something that neither of us had ever done. Suddenly we were hailed by the crew of a power boat on our starboard side. They exclaimed they had run out of gas and were drifting in toward the beach and asked if we could tow them. George and I were not aware that sail boats usually don't tow power boats and George said he thought the "law of the sea" dictated that assistance must be provided.

When we searched for a line that we could throw them, we could only find short dock lines and someone had plaited our longer lines into a neat looking but not helpful rope rug. I circled around explaining our dilemma to the hapless power boater when I felt movement under our hull and it soon became apparent that we were in the surf line, parallel to the beach and being propelled rapidly in that direction. Our mainsail was still up. We hit the beach about the same time as the power boat 100 yards away

The surf waves were substantial, driving our 7,000-pound keel into the sand. The waves continued crashing into our port side. I turned off the motor. It seemed no time at all before a well-built life guard clambered aboard and lowered our mainsail. Then, probably because of George's white hair, he grabbed George, threw him over his shoulder and waded through the surf onto dry land. I heard George ask him to please put him down.

I soon became aware of a powerful life guard boat rumbling just past the surf line. Another lifeguard dove over the side of their boat and swam ashore with a heavy-duty line. They hooked the line to our mast and cranked up their powerful boat. This tipped our boat onto its port side and pulled the heavy, buried, lead keel out of the sand and kept moving until our boat was past the surf line. These guys were magnificent and made me proud to be a tax-payer.

After I told them where our slip was located, they towed us there and got us situated. When I tried to check out our interior for problems, I found that we had a slow leak and water was gathering slowly in the bilge. I knew someone had to keeping pumping the bilge until daylight.

Marcia brought our son Buck(Lee) and his friend Curtis from Orange County and they pumped the bilge periodically all night until I set up an automatic pump the next day that could keep us afloat until we were able to get her into dry dock to repair the keel which had slightly separated from the hull, hence the leak.

We had many happier voyages to Catalina, San Clemente Island and San Diego in the years following and many good parties on the boat. My friend George never sailed the boat by himself, but did motor around Marina del Rey to restaurants etc. It was a great adventure.

SAD EPILOGUE

I first met Mr. Herbert Chance, as I stated in My First Sailing Voyage story, on December 7, 1941, three days after my eighth birthday. At that time the Nuway hot dog stand consisted of four stools with accordion folding doors. But I am told, that he started out some time before that with a push cart on the corner of Pico and Bundy in West Los Angeles.

As the years went by, he continually expanded his business into a large restaurant, with a separate rest room building, large parking lot, and a separate office where Mrs. Chance arrived regularly driving the latest model of Cadillac and wearing what looked like expensive jewelry. There was a good-sized cocktail lounge next door and we later realized that he eventually bought that too, so he owned the whole city corner.

Regrettably, Herbert Chance started hanging out in his cocktail lounge next door. We assume this after once seeing him appear to stagger across the parking lot and also reading the legal documents dealing with his demise. Mrs. Chance, Virginia, seemed to come there nearly every day that George and I stopped by for a chili dog, so we figured she did the books and the banking. Later, we saw Herbert Chance get into a new Mercedes, so they must have been doing alright.

The Los Angeles Times reported that on October 12, 1975, Mr. and Mrs. Chance were robbed and murdered in their Venice home by a group of men who had befriended Mr. Chance in the cocktail lounge next door to the Nuway. Dee Watson, an employee (we assume waitress) of the Chance-owned cocktail lounge was murdered a few hours later by the same men who were concerned that she could identify them. They are currently serving life without parole sentences.

A lengthy description of what occurred can be seen in the appeal filed by the murderers, *People v. McKinney,* wherein Mr. Chance is described as a drunk, so he had obviously made the mistake of drinking to excess. The autopsy of his body revealed an alcohol content of .22, nearly three times the legal limit. The inhumane methods these scum bags used in ending the lives of Mr. and Mrs. Chance, is more than frightening, shooting them multiple times in the head with their hands handcuffed.

During the 70's, before the murders, I met a private investigator named Chance who was Herbert's nephew and asked him about the possibility of obtaining the recipe for the chili. Not long after that, Herbert Chance was no more. A very sad ending of an American success story.

THE CASE OF THE MISSING TIRES

It was raining like hell when I got the call from the big law firm. Their clients were in the office, could I come right over. No problem, I said, but the congested traffic made me late. When we got into the meat of the problem, they soon forgot their annoyance.

They had a big tire plant over on Telegraph Road that covered 55 acres. You've probably seen it, passing on the Santa Ana Freeway. It's the place that looks like a medieval castle. They were losing inventory and couldn't figure it out. It seemed that most of the shrinkage occurred in their top-of-the-line tires which were wrapped in cellophane to make the customer realize he was getting something special.

I discussed placing an undercover operative in shipping and maybe one in the guard force. On weekends, the plant was locked up tight and devoid of personnel except for two guards. The guards were stationed in the back, away from Telegraph Road, and took turns patrolling the interior for an hour while the alternate guard watched the rear gate.

The client requested that we station a couple of surveillance units around the plant for the upcoming weekend. I said it was probably a waste of money and we should wait for the undercover to give us some clues. But the client was insistent. They were right.

We used one operative per car, and had one operative sit south of the plant on Telegraph Road while the other one was in the rear. The one in front could observe the two-block long driveway which traversed one side of the plant and led to a huge steel roll-up door which was closed and locked for the weekend. Our operative could not see the door itself because of the angle from his surveillance position.

About 9 o'clock Saturday night a large rented truck passed our position on Telegraph Road and pulled into the long driveway. Our operative was shocked to see the truck accelerate down the driveway, probably hitting 30 miles an hour as it came to the roll-up door. Instead of a crash, the truck disappeared inside. By the time our man moved forward, the door was closed. Our operative remained in position to watch the door.

Exactly one hour later, the door rolled up and the rental truck rolled out and away. We followed the truck to South Los Angeles where the driver parked it on the street, entered a darkened house and was not seen until the next morning. I scrambled our troops to cover this new development. We maintained surveillance on the plant and truck.

In the morning another man arrived in casual clothes. He and the driver opened the big back doors of the rental truck to reveal it was stacked to the roof with cellophane wrapped tires. There is a special way to stack tires which allows a larger number in a space than just piling one on top of another. These tires had obviously been loaded by someone who knew the tire business.

For the next two days, with the help of two other males, the driver delivered tires to various locations around South Los Angeles. Some went to private garages in back of residences and larger quantities went to gas stations. There was well over $20,000 worth of tires in this truck. Our investigators filmed all of the deliveries and obtained good ID shots of all of the conspirators including some of money changing hands. Later, we methodically identified each one of them. One was a guard at the plant.

The rental truck driver was a long-term employee who was off work from the plant, on a questionable disability claim. The two other fellows, who helped unload the tires at different times of the day, were both identified as employees at the plant. One had worked there for 27 years and was due for retirement.

We needed to establish a chain of evidence for a criminal conviction. Our clients reluctantly admitted that once these tires left the plant there was no way to prove they were missing from their inventory and therefore stolen. This is often the case with most manufactured goods. The tire company was required to keep elaborate records of the manufacture of each tire and actually put a separate identifying number on each tire to meet government requirements. But these numbers were never tied into an inventory system. We proceeded to place an undercover operative in the guard force. At three of the gas stations, we placed orders for odd-sized cellophane wrapped tires, figuring the station owners would ask the thieves to fill the order.

We needed to enter the plant and surreptitiously mark some tires. Our client did not dare make too many inquiries about the guard schedule, since at this point we were not sure if other guards were in on the conspiracy. We waited until our undercover guard was scheduled to work the night shift. Since most guards hate to make rounds, we told him to volunteer to make the other guard's rounds even though it was against the rules. Bill, the plant manager, and I arrived at the plant shortly after midnight. We opened the front door of the plant which was not alarmed and hoped we wouldn't run into the wrong guard on his rounds.

The inside of a tire plant is a dark and dirty place when the lights are on. It seemed even worse that night. We crept past the huge Banbury machines that mix the glop that becomes tires. Past the steel-built applying equipment and eventually into the warehouse area. As we were reaching the area where the stored cellophane wrapped tires were, we saw a flashlight and hid behind some tires as the guard went by.

We had trouble locating the odd-sized tires at first and I started marking everything in sight with my initials and the date. I used a special crayon which is invisible to the naked eye unless placed under an ultraviolet light. Bill signaled he had found the special sizes. I marked them too. I must have marked 200 tires. Bill was getting nervous. He feared we would be discovered and his presence in the plant at that hour would scare off the culprits. We nearly ran into a guard again as we were leaving. It is hard to imagine the size of this place unless you start creeping around in the dark. We later learned it was our undercover guard.

The next day I made an appointment to meet with the East Los Angeles Sheriffs and our client. Now, working with the coppers can be fun or can be frustrating. Regrettably, a great many policemen have an attitude about private investigators. Sometimes they seem to be looking for ways to reduce their workload by discouraging the filing of complaints. For this reason, I try to let the client make the first overture to get their attention and then bring them the whole case with a pink ribbon around it so they are obliged to cooperate.

However, the East Los Angeles Sheriffs were, and still are, extremely different from the start. They were pleased when we gave them reports identifying each suspect and what went down. And they were amazed when we showed them the films of stolen tires being unloaded all over town. "How the hell do you do this without being burned," asked one detective. I grinned and said, "This is what we do for a living." We told him the tires and inventory were marked and that we were going to keep up the surveillance until the truck showed up to steal some more. It was agreed that if it took an hour for the truck to load and we call the Sheriff's office immediately that would be enough time for them to get to the plant.

It was time for me to keep my operatives company on surveillance but we got blanked one weekend when nothing happened. The next Saturday was a winner, however, and the truck showed up again about 9 PM. We scrambled the sheriff. The felony car and two black and whites arrived 10 minutes before the truck was expected to leave. We sat down Telegraph Road until the truck came out and turned north. As before the roll-up door went down immediately after the truck came out.

The black and whites hit the red light before the truck got past the north end of the plant. The detectives politely asked the driver to open the back of the truck and read him his rights when they saw the loaded tires. One of my surveillance operatives drove the truck to the sheriff's station while I accompanied the detectives around to the back of the plant to the gate. The crooked guard was still returning from his rounds. He was unaware we had busted the truck. When he reached the gate they read him his rights and gathered him up. I told the other guard to call his boss but not to worry that he didn't have an associate. I said the plant is safer without them.

At the station the detectives placed the suspects inside a cell and then went out to the truck. I unlimbered my old hardwood case detective kit, then grabbed my battery-powered ultraviolet light. The back doors of the truck were opened and they had a felony car's lights shining inside. I asked him to turn off the headlights, then turned on my black light. The back of the truck looked like a Christmas tree as the ultraviolet light hit all of my initials on the cellophane. Almost half the load had my initials which clinched the chain of evidence.

It is always pretty sad to see some of the longtime employees do time and lose their pensions because they were greedy. I enjoy trying to catch them, but seeing lives ruined always makes me feel bad. That was all there was to this caper, but it was not the end of the missing tire problem for this client.

CLEM

We received an assignment to conduct a surveillance of a fellow in a rural community. I'll call him Clem. My investigator got a good look at him the first day of the two-day authorization. He looked awful. We called the client and said so and suggested we only do the one day. They thanked us for not wasting their money.

Two months later I got a call from the examiner who sounded angry and requested that I come to his office. I was a fairly new manager, having spent several years in the field as a cameraman/investigator. The examiner showed me a medical report from an independent medical examiner. The IME had asked the claimant a bunch of questions about his ability to perform normal activities. Clem had impressed the doctor with his recovery and said he could ride his bicycle 2 miles or more a day. That he no longer needed his cane. Clem had suffered a serious injury two years before, and had some residual disability including the limp which was obvious to the doctor. But instead of the usual story about all the things he couldn't do, this fellow was telling the doctor how great he felt.

The examiner was being pressured to settle the case by the claimant's lawyer. But the claimant wanted more to settle than the medical report's description of his abilities indicated. To placate my good client, I offered to conduct another day of surveillance for free. A different but equally experienced cameraman was assigned to the case. He saw Clem moving about his place and followed him into town. Clem's daughter drove the car and did all the loading of groceries. Clem kind of struggled along behind her leaning heavily on his cane.

My client had serious questions about the validity of our observations even though we had film to corroborate. He had another doctor examine Clem over the attorney's objections. Clem told this doctor he was doing fine, didn't need his cane but limped and was now riding his bicycle 5 miles a day. The claims examiner phoned to say he was looking for another investigative agency.

The next day I arrived at Clem's house myself. I went to his door and made a contact. He was using the cane as he answered the door. On previous surveillances, no contact had been necessary since he always came out before we needed to establish his presence. My investigators have reported they observed through binoculars that his bicycle was on the front porch.

As I pursued my contact subterfuge Clem came out onto his porch. It was then I noticed the bike had two flat tires and enough dirt accumulated around it indicated it had not moved in several months at best. I asked him if it was his bike and he said it was. Now it was my turn to be irritated with my client.

The punchline: Clem wanted his settlement so he could move back to Arkansas. He was willing to take less money to get the money soon. Several fellows at the union hall, experienced malingerers all, had told Clem that the judge would not approve a settlement when he was still recovering and obviously disabled. They said the only way he could get his money was to convince the doctors and judge that he had recovered and his condition was permanent and stationary.

A CLASSIC INSURANCE DEFENSE CASE

We call our surveillance investigators cameramen. Sometimes camera persons. Women can do the job fine, but the ones I've trained tend to get discouraged with the long hours and lack of social life. But that's another story.

The secret of success to being a cameraman is getting up early. The early bird catches the malingerer. Getting to an area before sun-up allows you to watch the neighborhood wake up and you can get a feel for how things are in case you have to spend the day there. Even if you are lucky and your subject takes you on a trip, getting there late might cause you to miss them leaving, and blow your whole day. Most camera jobs require you to start at sun-up, or just before, and work until dark. Filming is easier in daylight, but sunlight is not mandatory. The exception to quitting at sundown is when the subject is out and about instead of being at home.

The bulk of a cameraman's cases are insurance defense. Seeking malefactors who are attempting to defraud a company or insurance carrier by representing they are injured when they are not. Some dishonest claimants are content to sit home and do nothing, but many have other jobs or business or recreation in which they participate. Did you ever get on the freeway at five in the morning and wonder who the hell all the people are driving in both directions? Well, many are probably fraudulent claimants.

Private investigation is expensive. Claims handlers do not hire outside sub rosa investigation unless they are pretty sure they are dealing with a malingerer. So, there is a pretty good chance they are working at an undisclosed job, or otherwise active. The cameraman has to get to the claimant's house early to be able to follow him or her away to work, or other activity.

We received a surveillance assignment from a law firm that specialized in insurance defense. I will call the claimant Big Joe. I arrived at Big Joe's house before dawn. His Cadillac Coupe de ville was parked in front. The house was a two-story white frame. He lived there with his mother.

This was a liability case with the much-feared Melvin Belli's law firm on the other side. I say much-feared because the flamboyant Belli was famous for obtaining giant awards from juries.

Belli is a story in himself. He was married six times and even did some television acting. At his main office in the Barbary Coast section of San Francisco, he had a cannon on the roof and a flag pole. When he won a big case, he would fire off the cannon and hoist the Jolly Roger up the flag pole. I can't make these things up. Insurance defense lawyers called him Melvin Bellicose. His nick name was the King of Torts.

Belli had many celebrity clients including ZsaZsa Gabor, Errol Flynn, Chuck Berry, Muhammad Ali, the Rolling

Stones, Lana Turner, Tony Curtis and Mae West. It is rumored he won over $600 million in damages for his clients. He was also attorney for Jack Ruby who shot Lee Harvey Oswald after the assassination of President John F. Kennedy. But I digress.

Although Belli's headquarters is in San Francisco, he had a branch office in Beverly Hills. Big Joe had serious and legitimate injuries. While waiting for the attendant to bring his car in a downtown Los Angeles parking lot, the car went out of control in reverse, pinning Joe against a brick wall and rendering compound fractures of both legs.

Belli's office claimed Big Joe could not drive and was virtually a prisoner in his house with his aged mother having to care for him. Belli's settlement demand was astronomical. He relied on his reputation as "the King of Torts" to cower the other side into submission, sometimes, without a trial. There is no question that Belli is dangerous in court when he has a legitimately injured client, but there are a lot of other less famous lawyers as good or better. Still, my client was worried enough to hire us to conduct several days of surveillance.

Our company rules say that our cameramen have to make a contact on the claimant by 10 AM. If the subject is not home, the job is usually finished unless you know where to look for them and can find them in an hour. You may get another job, or you may be out of work for the day. Our agency is obligated to pay the operative mileage and travel time from our office to the subject's home and back. If you don't make a contact by 10 AM to establish the subject's presence, you're on your own for any additional time if there is no one home. I had a positive make from DMV on Big Joe's car, and since it was in front, I elected not to make a contact at 10 AM.

By noon I was getting antsy, so I phoned and spoke to his mother. She said he was in bed asleep, which was probably true, but not because of his injuries. I called the boss to check again and continued surveillance.

At 3:30 PM Big Joe came out of the house on crutches and I filmed him as he hobbled to his Cadillac at the curb, got in and drove away. I tailed him to Belli's Beverly Hills office and filmed him going in and out on his crutches. He looked like a guy who was recovering from two broken legs. But I also got pictures of him driving which he alleged he could not do. I figure the law firm was bankrolling him until the trial. Big Joe was probably picking up an advance.

He left the law office about 4:45 and drove east on Santa Monica to Crescent Heights then up and north over Laurel Canyon past Mulholland and over to the San Fernando Valley. He parked in front of the Blarney Stone, a popular watering hole on Ventura Boulevard which also serves pretty good chow. He mounted the sticks and crutched his way in the front door. I waited an hour before entering the back door of the Blarney Stone.

It was a hot, bright summer day in the Valley and the interior of the saloon was both cool and dark. I wanted to see what he was doing without calling too much attention to myself.

Before my eyes got accustomed to the dim interior, I was on top of him, seated at the end of the bar, and I tripped over his crutches which were sticking out into the aisle. Needless to say, he noticed me. I apologized and walked two thirds of the way down the long bar and swung my butt onto a stool. I ordered a beer and casually looked to my right. Big Joe was staring a hole right through me!

He soon forgot me as the bar started to fill up with regulars who all seemed to know him. His drink was Tuaca on the rocks. A few non-regular types, usually couples, would come in for a drink and dinner, but the bar trade all seemed to know each other. I nursed two beers and left. It was almost 7PM.

I was starved. I phoned the deli down the street and ordered a corn beef on rye to pick up in 10 minutes. When I got back Big Joe's caddy was still in front of the Blarney Stone. I called the boss at home and he told me to put him to bed and get back on him at seven the next morning. Now, it was about 11 PM. I took a chance and went for a hot chocolate. I was back in six minutes. He was still there.

Big Joe and some others came out at 2:15 AM and drove a block to Tiny Naylor's coffee shop for breakfast. At 3:40 AM he drove home and so did I. I had been up since 4:45 the previous morning. I slept for three hours, crawled out and got back on him a little after eight. I was an hour later than the boss instructed, but I figured Big Joe was tired too.

The Caddy was still in front. Big Joe came out about 4:30 in the afternoon. I was struggling to keep awake. He drove directly to the Blarney Stone and went in. I called the boss and he said to go inside and see what was happening. This time I went in the front door. Joe was holding court in the back telling raucous stories, laughing and pounding the bar while inhaling copious quantities of his Tuaca.

I had my beers, then went to the phone in the back door to order my corn beef from the deli. I ate in the car, then went back into the bar for another beer. Nothing changed. Big Joe was really obnoxious. Loud and nasty. It was a little surprising that they put up with him, because I could see some of the dinner crowd was annoyed by his noise. But he frequently bought a round for all the barflies and bragged about what he would do when he got his big insurance settlement.

About two 2 AM he came out with a guy and two women. They were all three sheets to the wind. They drove to a Turkish bath, but there must've been some problem getting the women in. They drove away again and pulled up in back of the car wash at Laurel Canyon and Ventura. Joe had a bottle which they seemed to be passing around and they were making plenty of noise so I knew nobody was getting laid. It was after 3 AM now and I was exhausted. My orders were to put him bed, so I dared not sleep.

About 3:30, I had had enough. I went to a payphone at the car wash and called the cops. I said I was a resident at a home in the tract that backed up to Ventura Boulevard. I said I wished to remain anonymous, but I described Big Joe's car and location and complained about the noise. In five minutes a black and white rolled up and two cops asked Joe to step out of the car. Now I thought, the obnoxious jerk was going to go to bed, even if it's in jail.

But the minute Big Joe swung the crutches out and tried to stand up, the coppers decided they wanted none of it. I could see them thinking about all the trouble and paperwork and potential civil liability to book a giant drunk on crutches. They took down the poop from his license and told him to go home, then left. Big Joe drove to Tiny Naylor's again, the bunch had breakfast and after breakfast, he went home. I was too tired to drive but I got home somehow.

We had film of Big Joe driving his car, which he claimed he couldn't do, as well as my testimony that he could sit on a barstool for hours instead of being housebound. But our client was concerned about the film of him on crutches, backfiring. When you show pictures in court, they must portray the claimant is a giant fake, so the jury wants to boo them out of the courtroom. The plaintiff's lawyer will make a big deal out of the fact that we follow the claimant around using words like spy, sneak, snoop, invasion of privacy, etc. They try to make it look like we are persecuting the poor claimant when in fact all we are trying to do is investigate the legitimacy of his claim.

Case law has always held that the defendant has a duty to investigate and bring the facts before the court. So, if your film is borderline, that is, not a dramatic contrast to what the plaintiff admits, it may not overcome the natural prejudice of the jury. Even though Big Joe was exaggerating his limitations a little bit, the fact of the matter was he had severe injuries, our insured was responsible, we admitted it, and he did need crutches to get around.

I reported Big Joe's conversations which I had overheard. The client lawyers decided they would like to know more about Big Joe and what he espoused. So, I was assigned to drop by the Blarney Stone every night after my regular day of surveillance, sip a beer or two and observe and listen to what Big Joe had to say. I made no effort to engage him in conversation although he did speak to me on occasion.

As I mentioned, Big Joe was a foul-mouthed individual who exhibited signs of paranoia from time to time. One night he grabbed me around the neck and started raving about being spied on saying "they're coming out of the clouds", whatever that meant. The mere weight of his arm nearly knocked me off the stool. Other than I was a fairly new face in the bar, he had no cause to suspect me. This soon passed and he was insulting someone else. He would say appalling things in a loud voice, particularly when a nice-looking woman would stray into the bar. "Boy I'd like to lay a four-pound tongue into that," he would say. Only his crutches saved him from Armageddon, big as he was.

As I fed the information back to our lawyers, they begin to drop tidbits about Big Joe in their settlement conversation with Belli's henchmen. I learned a number of incriminating things which his lawyers were unaware of. Big Joe admitted them to his lawyers and they wondered what else we knew that they didn't. So bottom line, my clients were able to settle for about 25% of the demand. This still gave Big Joe a six-figure jackpot, but he had to repay the advances and give Belli's office the one third or so that they always cut out for themselves. Our client was delighted to avoid the legal fees, the risk of a big sympathy verdict, and pay a reasonable sum. The film was never used. Needless to say, calling the cops on Big Joe so I could get some sleep did not appear in my report.

THE CASE OF THE TOP SECRET PLANS

The attorney who called me was a senior partner in a 100-lawyer firm in downtown Los Angeles. Bud was one of the founders of the firm and it bore his name. We had worked with Bud on a number of unusual cases in the past. He said he had a client with a special problem that I might be able to fix.

The client makes high-speed motion picture cameras for commercial use. Some are the kind that shoot a thousand frames per second. When you see the cornflakes pouring into the bowl or the slow-motion water drops on TV, it's usually his equipment. He also does a lot of contract work for the government. Some top-secret stuff like gunsight cameras for jet fighters.

As a taxpayer, I admire his method of doing business with the Navy and Air Force. When they get ready to come out with a new fighter, they give John the specifications for the camera they need. He designs a prototype at his own expense and if they like it, goes into production and makes 1500 or so of them. Because the R&D was privately funded, we were asked to do the investigation instead of the FBI.

The business is quite competitive and needless to say, the plans and prototypes are of the highest proprietary nature within the firm, not to mention the governments need for secrecy.

The plant and its location mirror the character of the founders, or at least one of them. They employ more than a hundred people in a single-story building that backs up to the Los Angeles River. There is bare land around the plant which is put to equestrian use. The chairman and president founded the company in a garage and never got used to the fact that they were millionaires. Chairman Dick is somewhat normal. But President John has a wild streak. He reminds me of the popular country-western song, "I've always been crazy but it kept me from going insane." I really like him.

When I first met John, he was wearing threadbare pants and a shirt that looked like a test for Consumer Reports. The omnipresent cigarette either dangled from his lips while he twisted and squinted to see or was wedged between brown-stained fingers. When he put his feet up on his big desk in his office, he displayed holes in the soles of both his tattered boots.

Later I found out he lived in the center of the large cemetery right across the river. To meet him at home, you had to enter the cemetery's wrought iron gates and wind around to get to his rambling ranch house just over the hill from the grave digging action. It was nestled in a hollow along a stand of eucalyptus trees. The sprawling ranch house fit John's persona like a glove. It's definitely lived in.

John is now married to a dark-haired beauty but he never misses the opportunity to mention how his ex-wife and her lawyer took him for a bundle. John's hobby and diversion is racing dirt bikes across the desert. He broke an ankle on one Baja race and rode his bike 70 miles to get medical attention. Diminutive in size, John is tough as nails and a character. John is also soft-hearted and generous to his friends. Not so charitable to his enemies. The less volatile Dick complements John to a T making it a perfect partnership.

They laid out the story. Bill, one of their more promising young engineers had been approached by a former employee named Herman. This guy had somehow found out that John's company was nearly finished with the plans and prototype for a new gunsight camera for the F104. Herman told Bill he represented a principal who did not wish to disclose his identity. He said his client was also a camera manufacturer and offered to pay a considerable sum for the plans and substantially more if he could get his hands on the prototype. He also said that Bill could quit his present position after the theft and Herman's client would give him an important position at a higher salary. Bill was no fool. He went straight to John.

After I talked John out of kidnapping and castrating Herman, he agreed we should play this fish to find out who the alleged client was.

John said he had his suspicions, but he would let me do my job without any suggestions. The message was clear. No rock would be left unturned until we nailed the alleged client. I explained to John we would probably need to record some of our machinations with Herman so John dutifully accompanied me to see the District Attorney - frayed pants, holey boots and all. We were assigned an excellent prosecutor. Bart was the best technical trade secret expert in the office. Out of 5,000 lawyers that ain't bad. He quickly grasped our dilemma, opened a file and authorized us to make telephone and other recordings of our conversations with Herman without Herman's knowledge.

I never cease to be amazed at the number of lawyers and other smart people who don't know that it is unlawful to record a conversation in California, telephone or otherwise, without every party to the conversation having knowledge. Big Daddy Jesse Unruh left us with that gem of a new state law after he was embarrassed when a political enemy recorded his private conversation while Speaker of the House. The federal statutes only require that one party to the conversation have knowledge, but in California it's now all parties.

Wiretaps of course are only by court order. I have had to decline State Bar Association Presidents requests to bug phones. Clients and investigators frequently have to be reminded there is no point in obtaining evidence which is inadmissible. That type of evidence is often only obtained by breaking the law which makes no sense either.

Bill, the young engineer, didn't want to be our undercover man. He pleaded for us to dupe in an investigator in his place and offered to make the introduction. It was no accident that Herman picked Bill to approach. Bill's expertise and responsibility was considerable. There was no way we could make an investigator into a knowledgeable engineer and plant him without tipping Herman off. John promised Bill that he would remember him in his will, and Bill was reluctantly dragged into our investigation.

We gave Bill a crash course and started recording his return calls to Herman. Bill played hard to get but slightly interested in the bribe money. Herman made many incriminating admissions over the phone, but steadfastly resisted allowing Bill to meet or know the identity of his client, who we had decided to nickname Big.

We put a tail on Herman for a few days and he eventually met a man for lunch at the Red Lantern on Chandler Boulevard, in North Hollywood. We tailed this guy and identified him. We suspected he was Big. I was unprepared for John's reaction when I told him the name of the guy who was lunching Herman. He jumped up from his desk and shouted, "That son of a bitchin' mother f----r. I figured he would be behind this."

I mumbled something about thanks for telling me.

It turns out that Big worked for John and Dick for 12 years. He had been the shop superintendent. He was a capable and trusted employee, who had authority to purchase tools and equipment and sign for anything. About 10 years into his employment Big asked John if he could open his own small machine shop on the side doing work that would in no way compete or conflict with John's camera manufacturing. Good guy John gave his, okay.

Two years later, someone noticed a lot of tools missing from the inventory. As a matter of fact, special items had been purchased that no one had ever seen in John's shop. John heard rumors that Big was trying to sell cameras he had made in his shop in direct conflict with what he promised John he would do. John figured it was time for a visit.

He arrived at Big's shop armed with purchase orders which Big had signed and receipts for tools purchased for John's company which contain descriptions and serial numbers of many expensive items. By this time, he was not surprised to find Big had completely outfitted his shop with tools stolen from John, many of which were ordered new and never placed in John's plant at all.

Big pleaded for mercy. John relented. Instead of having Big prosecuted for theft, he fired Big and accepted partial restitution for the stolen items.

Now several years had passed and Big had not learned his lesson or been grateful for the reprieve. Yes, John was pissed.

Bill continued to talk to Herman on the phone and agreed to sell him a set of plans for five grand. They met in a grocery store parking lot and we filmed and recorded the exchange of money for the plans which looked real, but were phonies. Herman pressed for the prototype.

Bill countered that if he stole one, he would definitely have to leave his job and he wasn't about to change jobs without knowing who Herman's client was. Herman finally relented. Herman wouldn't identify Big there, but said he would bring Big to Bill's home when Bill had acquired the proto-type. Big would pay Bill for the prototype and discuss future job plans at that time.

Several District Attorney investigators were assigned to take down Big and Herman at the appropriate time. Because Bill lived in the Burbank jurisdiction, we advised Burbank Police of our plans. They said they would provide a black-and-white patrol car as a backup for the bust. Burbank has a very fine police department and detective staff who have always been very helpful.

On the final afternoon there were a bunch of us in Bill's house. The District Attorney's investigators wired Bill for sound and dusted the prototype so it would pick up prints. They poked holes in the drywall and retired to the bedroom as we saw Big and Herman drive up. Bill answered the door and Herman introduced Big to him. Since Bill had been hired after Big was fired, Bill had never met him.

They sat down in the living room and Big admired and handled the prototype putting his prints all over it. Bill got them to discuss the fact that Big was buying stolen property and Big produced an envelope of cash which Herman began to count out.

When we had enough on tape to convince any idiot of what was going down, the District Attorney's detectives jumped out of the bedroom with guns drawn. This was unnecessary, but standard procedures until the bad guys are frisked and handcuffed. Besides it was fun and scared the shit out of the opposition. I have seen many a fellow wet his pants, or worse when the cops bring out their guns and shout something subtle and polite like POLICE! FREEZE!

The District Attorney's people did a good job. We eventually got a conviction to a lesser count and some restitution. Big did little time but got a bunch of probation since it was his first offense. The same for Herman. It still cost John money that he couldn't recover to pay my bill. But I think he thought it was worth it.

I went to see him the other day. He's still living in the cemetery, and his employees just gave him a new trailer to haul his dirt bikes around for his birthday. He is 60 something and grizzled as ever. A reminder that one of the most satisfying aspects of being an investigator is the fun of sticking your nose in other people's business, and making lifelong friends out of your clients.

I may be cynical, but I bet Big and Herman are out there somewhere trying to screw somebody else as we speak.

JASPER WILLIAM McCLAIN

Even private eyes have relatives. Some of mine are outstanding.

My grandfather was born August 7, 1866, in Illinois, the year after the end of the Civil War. His family soon moved to Exira, Iowa, where his father farmed in addition to being a renowned horse doctor without portfolio. His father was Thomas Jefferson McClain. Since he is gone, we get away with calling him T.J. No one ever called my grandfather by his name, but rather he was always known as "J.W. McClain".

J.W. always said he had done enough manual labor by the time he was 16 to last a lifetime. He was driving a team pulling a walk-behind plough when he was only 13. T.J. apparently worked his sons considerably. Since J.W. was already 67 when I came along, I never saw him wear anything but a suit with a vest.

He obtained a job selling buggies with "the Spalding Company." He was good at it. Experiencing some sale success, J.W. and his partner Cowan, formed their own company selling custom made buggies and carriages bearing the Cowan and McClain label. They had a unique assembly-line system of selling that was very successful.

In those days, everything went by train. The pair would have a freight car load of buggies dropped off in a farm town to start their route. Their advance man would arrive on the passenger train. He would hire locals to unload the box car and assemble the buggies while he was putting up posters announcing a buggy sale the following day.

The next day, J.W. and his partner arrived on the passenger train and sold the buggies. The advance man had caught the same passenger train to the next town where a freight car of buggies had been dropped off and he repeated the hiring and assembly as before.

J.W always liked California weather and set up a carriage dealership in downtown Los Angeles much like Cadillac would do these days. He married a handsome Exira school teacher named Mary Grace Green. Grace traveled to the Northwest Territories and elsewhere with him.

This marriage produced two sons, my uncles Garland and Homer born in 1902 and 1904 respectively.

Around 1900, having amassed some cash in the days before income tax, J.W. started speculating on land and purchased 4,000 acres in southern Alberta which he sold about a year later more than doubling his money. Properties that he bought and soon sold in southern Alberta included the Mendenhall Ranch, Butte Farm, Goose Neck Farm, and Prairie Farm. The Province of Alberta was not established until 1905.

In 1904, against the advice of bankers in Lethbridge, J.W. purchased a township, that's 36 sections, or six square miles of prairie land, from the Canadian Pacific Railway in an area now known as Nobleford, where I was later raised. Charles S. Noble represented the railroad as realtor and later bought four of the sections where the town of Nobleford and Noble Farm now stand.

Defying the skeptics who said the area was not fertile, J.W. broke 450 acres of sod using four-bottom plows behind three teams of eight mules each. He planted fall wheat and the virgin soil yielded 45 bushels to the acre. There were no elevators so his crew accumulated huge piles of grain before hauling it to the railhead in Granum where he had to sign for box cars. When other would-be farmers saw the huge piles of wheat, they flocked to buy acreage and J.W. sold several sections for three times his purchase price, then continued to break and farm the rest.

J.W. eventually built a two-story family home in 1906 and several outbuildings including a race horse barn with a hardwood dance floor on the second story where he later held community barn dances. He also created a race track for training his race horses. He named his ranch, *The California Stock Farm.*

Tragedy struck in 1910 when wife Mary Grace contracted meningitis and passed away. She was only 38. His young sons, Garland and Homer accompanied J.W. on the train to Exira, Iowa, where she is buried with an impressive monument which we have visited. J.W. built a home on 39th Street in Los Angeles and hired a couple to care for his two boys when he was on the road.

At a saltwater plunge in Ocean Park, California, J.W. struck up a friendship with the cashier of the bath house, Ida Montgomery. Her father, Albert Gibbs Montgomery, my great-grandfather, was born in 1843 in Charleston, South Carolina.

When the Civil War began, he enlisted in the South Carolina 23rd Infantry fighting for the South in seven battles. He was twice wounded. Things were not good for South Carolinians after the war, so in 1868 he joined his father who had earlier moved to California. Albert married Helen Maither and they had four children. Thanks to Abe Lincoln, he was finally able to homestead 160 acres around 1896 in Topanga Canyon, California, although initially Rebel veterans were denied the opportunity, unlike the "damn Yankees."

In 1912, J.W. married Ida Mae Montgomery, in Santa Monica, California. Ida took over raising Garland and Homer and they had two more children, my father Irving and Aunt Maxine. All four of J.W.'s children graduated from Manual Arts High School.

J.W. raised and raced horses from 1909 to 1923. These were trotting horses, pacers and trotters. He raced them from Edmonton, Alberta to San Diego and from Vancouver to Ottawa, Ontario. He had two world's records.

J.W.'s three brothers and a sister, including his parents, moved from Iowa to Alberta and J.W. helped them all get started.

As each of his children graduated from high school in Los Angeles, they moved to Alberta. Homer and Garland were first and purchased some land before also purchasing a section each from their father. J.W. then sold Irving and Maxine each 960 acres on a no-interest 20-year payout.

My parents took me up there when I was a year old. My Dad bought a tar paper covered cook trailer from an oil drilling outfit, set it on wooden blocks, and that was our home. Periodically he would cut a hole in a wall and add a room. He also built a large Quonset style machine shed and other buildings. We had some pigs, which we ate.

Then Irv lost his head and purchased 3,000 chickens in 1,000 chick batches. Now, our weekends were spent cleaning eggs. But we had lots of delicious fried chicken.

Irv's asthma from the wheat dust worsened so he leased his farm to Maxine and Garland. After Irv and I moved our belongings to California and a brief stint in college, I enlisted in the U.S. Army Airborne. After boot camp, the Army sent me to Georgia for parachute training, but sent my entire training company to Korea. At a USO dance in Columbia, South Carolina, I cut in on junior hostess Marcia Bankhead who was dancing with some infantry guy. We were married a year later. At this writing we have been married for 68 years and have eight great-grandsons. After spending most of my working life in California, our life together continues near our family in Arizona.

SOUPS ON

If you are like me, you have eaten this company's product your entire life. In the nineties, we received an assignment to investigate a drug problem at their huge soup preparation plant in Ohio. Since they employed three shifts, it was a large assignment. To work it, we installed an investigator undercover in their workforce on each of the shifts.

In this small town, I'm sure more than 50% of the inhabitants worked for the soup company. The police department consisted of nine employees and most probably had relatives in the plant. As a result, to keep our presence a secret, we didn't advise the police chief we were there. We did tell the DEA and the Bureau.

The client's company headquarters was on the east coast but we dealt primarily with local management who were realistic to work with. After a few months we had identified 62 employees who were either using drugs or selling them in the plant. All of the suspects were interviewed by a separate team of our interviewers and signed confessions obtained from nearly every one of them.

We don't make personnel recommendations to our clients. In this case when they asked, we shared that many of our clients only disciplined the users but sometimes terminated the sellers, which in this case was less than a dozen employees. Local management thought this was the way they wanted to handle it since they wanted to keep a workable relationship with the union.

But the home office wanted something more draconian. Nearly every one of the 62, most of whom were only users, were terminated. Even with a 1,000 plus employee work-force, and even though we had their confessions, this was too much for the union to swallow. They sued both the soup company and Krout & Schneider, Inc.

Our workable, friendly relationship with the Ohio man-agement team went out the window when their east coast lawyers got into it. Their primary goal was to lay off the liability on to someone else. That's what lawyers do. So, now our client is suing Krout & Schneider saying that we did a poor job of investigation and our firm is the reason they have been sued. Under the terms of our liability insurance policy, we were not allowed to discuss the particulars of the investigation with anyone or they would refuse to provide coverage.

One of our other clients happened to be a major TV network. We worked several jobs for them including the Menendez brothers murder investigation. It was our firm that discov-ered where the brothers purchased the shotguns they used to kill their parents in Beverly Hills. But that's another story.

The TV network wanted us to provide a story and we had to decline. They had a weekly one-hour program called 20/20. They sent a crew to Ohio and interviewed several of the employees that had been terminated for drugs. They filmed the ex-employees in their homes surrounded by family and each, including two of the primary drug dealers, related a tearful tale of woe about being wrongfully terminated by the soup company and persecuted by the investigators who cruelly accused them.

The TV people continued to bug us asking for a statement. Even though this would have been our chance to publicly prove our case, we had to decline. So, the TV network sent a camera team and filmed our office building which had our company name prominently displayed. From the back side of our building, they took long distance shots of our front door and office area where again our name was displayed. Their editors cleverly interspersed this film into the undenied, tearful interviews of the employees who had been terminated and their families. The program repeatedly stated that our firm refused to provide a statement which I am sure the audience would construe as our guilt of doing something wrong.

The union went all out with their lawsuit and their lawyers discovered our firm had not advised the police chief that we intended to do the undercover investigation. They discovered an obscure sentence in the Ohio state licensing statutes, that said the police chief should be advised in advance. Although we had advised the DEA and the FBI of what we were doing, we had purposely not advised the chief who, along with other members of the nine-man police force, probably had relatives working in the plant.

The small town did not have a full-time city attorney, but we were contacted by their part time attorney who represented the town. He explained that the union was giving him heat to take legal action against our firm. Although he was sympathetic to why we had tried to maintain confidentiality he had to do something. He advised if an officer of our firm would appear to plead guilty, they would accept $1,000 to settle the case. My son, Mark McClain who is a vice president, flew to Ohio, pled on behalf of the firm, and provided the cashier's check. Of course, this was fertile ground for the TV program.

Ultimately, our insurance company took part in a settlement conference and requested that an officer of our firm participate. I flew to Toledo. I let them know we didn't appreciate being castigated for doing our job correctly, but that's what happened. The company was forced to take back nearly all of the terminated employees to placate the union. If they had only terminated the employees who were selling the drugs, this probably wouldn't have happened. I still purchase and eat their soup.

AN IN-DEPTH PERSONAL INVESTIGATION

An emissary from the chairman of a large electronics man-ufacturer in Japan, comes to our Los Angeles office. This company is well known in the United States and I have some of their very upscale gear, which is very high quality. VCRs, CDs, players, etc.

The chairman's beautiful daughter has been going to college in the United States. She has fallen in love with an American male student that she met at the Santa Barbara college. The chairman wants to know everything there is to know about this fellow.

We explain to the extremely shy, bowing and smiling em-issary that we will need a retainer. He whips out a passel of traveler's checks. None of us have ever seen $1,000 travelers checks before.

We only requested a twenty-five-hundred-dollar retainer to start, but we received three grand because the shy fellow didn't have anything smaller and we didn't want to embar-rass him any further. He was anticipating at least $10,000.

This background investigation was like a fairytale. These two young people were unofficially the most handsome couple on the campus and madly in love. The blonde Adonis was not only from a wealthy family himself, but he was also a war hero pilot-type with a number of medals. Both young people were A students. We could not find one derogatory thing about the young man. He could care less about her money and could have had his pick of girls on campus.

It's gratifying to be able to report some good news for a change, The investigative report was sent to Japan. Unfortunately, we don't know what happened after we did our work. The chairman got a small refund.

TAPE PIRACY

Before the Bloods and the Crips, there weren't many real gangsters in Los Angeles and there never have been. Mickey Cohen and Bugsy Siegel are some of the more notable characters, but they never really were able to operate here like they do on the East Coast. The "Hats" of the Los Angeles Police Department, as they were nicknamed, harassed the hell out of them for years before anyone was concerned about probable cause.

Mickey, Bugsy, Meyer Lansky, and Moe Green in Las Vegas were "Jews" who carved out their own niches without too much trouble from the "Guineas." The true Sicilian types are few and far between. Since I got into the investigation business, there are only a few guys whose names end in vowels who have achieved minor notoriety in the press in Los Angeles. There have been a few contract killings in Los Angeles, but again, with the exception of Bugsy's shotgun killing, not many. So, when we get the average criminal case to work for a corporation, we seldom think of Mafia as a possibility.

When the San Francisco law firm pegged us to handle one of the first known tape piracy cases in the 70's there wasn't even any criminal statute on the books that could be used to prosecute. Civil action was doing a limited job while the record companies lobbied to change the Penal Code.

Our client was a record company subsidiary of the big three network, which was a subsidiary of a conglomerate with the same name as the record company. Confusing? That's what their canine logo thought looking into the phonograph.

The problem involved 8-track tapes, which had just rocketed into prominence. Cassettes and CDs were not on the market yet. Copious quantities of 8-track knockoffs were springing up at swap meets and small record stores all over the place. Our client had little to go on.

We started by canvassing the swap meets and outlets for pirate tapes. When we found someone dealing in quantity, we put them under surveillance and tried to identify their supplier. This was labor-intensive and we never did see a delivery being made where we could follow the truck back to a supplier. When we did see a delivery go down, the truck driver usually made two or three more deliveries, then dropped the truck at a rental yard and went home.

One swap meet vendor was visited by a lone man in a big new car who didn't look like he belonged to the seller's circle of friends. We followed this guy and kept him under surveillance. In addition to visiting various shops, stores and swap meets, he drove to two separate high-speed duplicating operations one in the South Bay and the other in the San Fernando Valley. In both instances, the little companies were located in small, light-industrial centers, the kind with rollup aluminum doors and 3,000-foot interiors. Bosses of these companies were young men in their late 20s or early 30s who had been recruited from the legitimate record industry. Someone had set them up with the capital to purchase the latest high-speed duplicating equipment. They staffed their shops with young people and were instantaneously in business. They had a ready market for all they could produce and didn't have to worry about sales and marketing.

We followed every employee and identified who they were, where they lived and developed background information on each. It soon became evident that persons unknown had provided a substantial amount of money to set these young people up in business and they were all making good money. The machines cost over $10,000. They all knew better than to ask where the stuff was going or who really controlled the distribution. We had to prepare a civil case which would prove that the tapes they were producing were in fact pirated copies of the original recordings. A chain of evidence needed to be created from the original to the phony copy.

To do this, the record company brought the producers of each album to their Hollywood headquarters on Sunset Boulevard. Some of these people were in New York, Nashville, and other places and they had to fit this visit into busy schedules. Each provided affidavits stating they were present when the original recording was cut, that they listened to a copy of the record album and initialed same, and that they had listened to the pirated 8- track, initialed it, and then attested that the pirate tape was a reproduction of the original recording.

I must say this was the most fun part of the investigation for me. We met in an executive office, then trooped down the hall to a compact sound studio which was equipped with the biggest speakers I have ever seen, all battleship gray in color, plus other zoftic equipment.

They would put the recordings on the turntable and crank up the volume. I expected these guys to be pretty blasé about this music since they had created it and no doubt heard it many times. Instead, they seemed to get excited playing the records through these monster speakers.

The best was Elvis's man who flew in from Nashville. Elvis Presley had just made his comeback in Las Vegas, looking trim and fit. The album, which I still have, was a live Las Vegas performance. The piece de resistance was a seven minute and 30 second cut of "Suspicious Minds." I had heard the studio recording of the song but it in no way compares to the wild, live version. So here we are in this little room with these big speakers and you could feel the woofers radiate through your bones. We all started jumping around and the man from Nashville was the craziest of all. These guys love their music. I just wish Elvis had been there.

Continuing our surveillance on Mr. Big Car, we tailed him to an office in Mid-Wilshire which seems to be the headquarters for the distributors. No tapes ever came there. We later learned the wise guys had WATs Lines, so there would not be a record of any calls. The doors were always locked and you couldn't see in. If you knocked on one door, a door would open down the hall and a guy would gruffly ask what you wanted. No matter what we tried, no manner of subterfuge could get us inside.

The guy with the big car, who we later learned, was a small-time hood, would visit the production facilities, then go to the Wilshire office. He also made the rounds of local bandit distributors and some swap meets. Periodically a U-Haul type truck would arrive at the production plants and load up quickly. Some of the trucks delivered locally while others headed out of state. There was no connection between the trucks and their drivers and the production lines. After the local deliveries, the rental truck was returned to the rental yard. The driver then went home, probably to await a call for the next day's instructions. The next day, he would rent another truck.

Because we had no criminal offense to charge them with our clients had to file a civil suit and ask for injunctive relief to shut down the two reproduction operations. We swooped down with subpoenas and served everyone in sight. Key players who ran or weren't there when we arrived, were served at home. We were somewhat surprised at the fear which our papers created in these workers.

One kid, a truck driver, lived in the Venice area. We tailed him away from his crash pad and watched as he chained his racing bike to the railing at Santa Monica pier. When he walked back to his bike, we served him. He dropped the papers and took off running. Three days later the bike was still chained to the pier.

Just like the East Coast, the mob seldom uses muscle on citizens, because the public will call for their heads. But they do employ enforcers to keep other crooks in line. But at that point, we still didn't realize we were dealing with organized crime. Restraining orders effectively shut down the plants and we kept them under surveillance to be sure nothing was removed.

Our clients from San Francisco associated themselves with a Hollywood entertainment law firm and the subpoenas we served ordered ten 10 people to appear for their depositions at the Hollywood law firm's office.

The schedule called for a deposition each morning and afternoon for a week. The meter was running as two lawyers from the San Francisco firm waited patiently to take the depositions of people who never showed up. Wednesday afternoon they called me to say they were suspicious of a van which had been parked in front of the law firm's offices all week with someone inside. I assured them they were probably paranoid but we would look into it.

They gave me the license number and I ran the plate, as we say in the business. It came back to a some-what known Los Angeles hood, one of two brothers who made up the handful of known Mafia wise-guys in this area. Apparently, he had been engaged by the distribution guys to handle enforcement around town and he obviously was known on site by the "subpoenaed 10."

We were amazed he would drive his own vehicle, registered to himself at his home. But we figured the witnesses knew this man and this van was the prop needed to discourage their attendance. Only one of the 10 showed up for his deposition and he claimed to know nothing, which was probably almost true.

So, the bottom line of this operation was simple: The wise-guys controlled an elaborate distribution system using their WATS lines (Wide Area Telephone Service – a flat rate line). They hired drivers and paid them cash to rent trucks, make the deliveries, then go home and mind their own business. The ring- leaders implied trouble or job loss on these easily intimidated young people to keep them in line without worrying about LAPD. They conned people with some record production expertise into thinking they were going to make a bundle by being in business for themselves. They brought in the expensive machinery and got production underway very quickly.

The distribution set up people were totally separated from the production people except for the trucks which picked up and distributed the merchandise. When we busted an operation, they could simply find some more eager types with the requisite skills and install more equipment in a rented building. The equipment paid for itself in short order, thanks to the fact they had no overhead for the artists, orchestras, recording studios or advertising.

Soon after our work ended, the State Legislature added a statute to the California Penal Code to put some teeth in our bite. 8-track tapes went the way of the Edsel, but our clients were joined in the never-ending battle which still goes on. Counterfeit goods of all types, usually manufactured overseas, but sometimes, in our own country.

MY FIRST (AND LAST) KIDNAPPING INVESTIGATION

On November 22, 1960, San Diegan Tony Alessio was kidnapped.

Tony Alessio had seven brothers who were all involved in "business" in the San Diego and Tijuana, Mexico area. Most notably the Agua Caliente Race Track in Tijuana. From 1960 to 1963, they operated the Hotel del Coronado along with several restaurants and cocktail lounges including the Kona Kai Club. They were involved in the taxi, trucking, real estate and sea food businesses.

The Alessio family's background reflects many famous and infamous names in San Diego's history, like C. Arnholdt Smith and newspaper publisher James Copley. John Alessio appears to be the major domo of the brothers and ran the Agua Caliente Race Track in Tijuana. John had access to lots of cash and was the most prominent of the group.

He had relationships with both California Governors Edmund G. "Pat" Brown and Ronald Reagan. John who bragged he started out as a shoe shine boy, later built the Fifth Avenue Financial Center replete with a 13-story high-rise with a fancy restaurant, Mr. A's, on top. John even allegedly convinced the "government" to build the Coronado bridge so they could discontinue the ferry service to the island. Although the Alessio family was very prominent and admired as successful business people, they occasionally brushed with the law.

At one time, two of the brothers were convicted of tax evasion, paid $10,000 fines, and served relatively short prison sentences. Because they had women and other perks delivered to their cells they were convicted of bribing the prison officials and drew some more time for that. But the San Diego community seemed to accept that people in their business, particularly the race track, were required to associate with the criminal element. So, despite some seemingly sordid episodes, they were a prominent San Diego family

On November 22, 1960, four crooks headed by Frank Marrone, kidnapped Tony Alessio and held him blindfolded and hand cuffed. They initially demanded $600,000 but later agreed to reducing the ransom to $200,000. They told Tony's wife that if any attempt was made to mark the ransom money, they would send Tony's head to her in a box. The money was paid by John Alessio in a duffel bag.

Shortly, Frank Marrone and the others were arrested. Marrone admitted they used two revolvers, one of which was allegedly in a storm drain in Van Nuys, north of Los Angeles.

Maurice "Truck" Hannah, manager of the Los Angeles office of Krout & Schneider, received the assignment to attempt to locate one of the revolvers. Truck and I drove to the Van Nuys intersection and I donned my trusty paint covered coveralls and crawled into the storm drain. Sure enough, I located the gun wrapped in newspaper in the concrete drain. That was the extent of our investigation. Some months later, I was subpoenaed to appear in Superior Court in San Diego. After waiting for a few hours in the hallway, I was dismissed and advised my testimony would not be needed.

Although he originally pleaded guilty, Marrone later filed an appeal wherein he claimed that Tony Alessio was not the victim, but allegedly part of a conspiracy to extort money from John Alessio and the race track. This amazing claim is outlined in "San Diego Police Historical Association" on-line. Frank Marrone lost the appeal.

GETTING TO MOUNT OLYMPUS

I was working late in my office at Olympic and Union. When I came down to the garage, my new 1971 Buick Riviera was gone along with a triple turret 16mm camera, my .38 revolver, my gym bag and miscellaneous other stuff. The car, but not my stuff, was recovered in Beverly Hills four days later. I made a claim on my homeowner's insurance for $707.00. I learned a lesson to always read the terms of your insurance policy before you make a claim. It's also a good habit to read the policy when you first buy it.

When the adjuster called to make an appointment, I told him I was coming to his building to pick up an assignment, so I would come to him. I figured it should be a routine claim and maybe they would appreciate my courtesy.

They sent me a check for $107 saying most of the stuff was "tools" that I used in work, and therefore was not covered. Insurance companies are not appreciative.

When I was complaining about this to my lunch buddies, my friend "Buffalo" Bob Smith the lawyer, said I should sue them, and he offered to represent me. I said okay but wondered what he would be able to pull off to win.

Buffalo first subpoenaed their file, then deposed the claims examiner for two hours. Then he deposed the claims supervisor for two hours, and then subpoenaed the claims manager. At this point, the Vice President of Claims, a fellow Bob went to law school with, became aware of the lengthy depositions. He called Buffalo and asked what the hell was going on with this mickey mouse claim. Bob told him that they had pissed McClain off. The VP offered $1,500 to settle. I accepted.

I received a letter from Buffalo with the check enclosed and his bill for $30 which was his out of pocket for the filing fee. His letter said that if I should ever have need for a lawyer in the future, to please call another firm. I still have that letter. I put the check in the bank.

Marcia and I had been thinking about moving from Cypress in Orange County and relocate closer to the office in Los Angeles. Our major problem had been no extra money for a deposit until we sold our current home. After deposit of the $1,500 check, we began searching an area known as Mount Olympus where they were building new homes in the Hollywood Hills. We soon found a house that we were quite interested in making an offer on. The price was $90,000. When I asked the salesman how much the deposit was, he replied it was $1,500. That was just what we had, thanks to Buffalo. We sold that house 13 years later for $465,000.

Bob was married to Helen, who he called Sweetheart. They were our very good friends. Sweetheart's Aunt Toni had recently passed away and left her Hollywood Hills home to Helen. After they sold that home, Bob had a few hundred thousand in cash which he needed to invest. Apparently, someone gave him bad investing advice that resulted in a small financial loss which hurt more because it was Helen's inheritance.

One day, shortly thereafter, I was driving Buffalo Bob and his partner George Brownfield to lunch when I mentioned Security Pacific bank was dragging their feet on a $350,000 construction loan, I had applied for to build our new home in Fallbrook. When I called Bob that afternoon as he requested, he offered to loan me the $350,000.00, on an unsecured promissory note, which he did, and which I paid back at the going rate of interest. He obviously trusted me.

Buffalo passed away in January 2004 leaving me as the Trustee for his estate, a task that I handled without fee for seven years before turning it over to his son Mark.

One day as we were having lunch, I had asked him why, with that office full of lawyers, he picked me to be his Trustee. He responded with a smile, "It's because you're so damned honest."

RUNAWAYS #1

The governor's office in New Mexico calls to ask if we can handle an assignment for a wealthy and influential Hispanic constituent. Their 14-year-old daughter has run away.

In the past her family indulged her by flying to Los Angeles to let her attend rock concerts. She is tired of "dumb old New Mexico" and yearns for the city lights and the action. The Sunset Strip is in full bloom: Whiskey a Go Go, Gazzaris, etc.

The parents come to town and take a penthouse suite in the tower at the Beverly Wilshire. We meet and I get a picture and description. She is a young teenager with a mature body. There seems to be no particular person she would come to see. They are not even sure she is in Los Angeles. I try to make the clients feel they are in good hands, but not raise their expectations. LA is 1,000 square miles of city filled with a few million people.

We start canvassing the motels on the Sunset Strip among other places. The law says they are not supposed to rent to anyone under 18 and are to ask for ID. To nobody's surprise, we have no luck. The parents are getting antsy. Money is no object.

We put six surveillance units into the Hollywood area covering Hollywood Boulevard, Santa Monica and Sunset Boulevards. My man Eli Chavira is a disarming crackerjack, Hispanic investigator. He is cruising Sunset Boulevard when the girl comes out of a flophouse motel, walks to the edge of the street, and sticks out her thumb. Eli makes her immediately. He offers her a ride and she accepts so he picks her up.

She wants to go to the San Fernando Valley to watch the cruisers on Van Nuys Blvd. Eli says okay but he has to make a call. It's the middle of the day, she has apparently checked out of the motel and is wearing her backpack. I tell Eli to take her directly to the Beverly Hills Police Department. I call the parents and ask them to meet me there.

They are reunited. We are heroes. Blind luck. Hopefully she won't run away again, but they usually do.

RUNAWAYS #2

A respected insurance defense lawyer calls, very distraught. I've been working with him for years. We are not pals, but he trusts me and thinks I have ability and can keep my mouth shut. His 15-year-old daughter Stacy has run away. He brings his wife to our office.

I see why the kid left. The mother has no rapport with her daughter and probably never will. The lawyer is a nice guy, but I think she wears the pants. Routine at home is for him and his wife to have three martinis as soon as he gets home. They don't understand the daughter. They have already contacted the daughter's friends. None will admit knowing where she is.

My ace female operative is Kathleen Kenny, a gutsy, smart investigator and a blue jeans kind of gal. She has made a bundle in real estate during the time she worked for me after being dumped by an ex-husband and left with no money and no credit. Kathleen later sailed around the world in a 27-foot sloop and wrote several commercially successful books on navigation and sailing. But that's another story.

Kathleen sets up a subterfuge to interview teenagers to talk about their troubles. She targets a group of Stacy's friends and establishes a rapport never mentioning Stacy. After a few sessions, the girls tell Kathleen about Stacy. They don't know where she is, but she contacts them from time to time. They say she is living with some hippies in a van.

Kathleen plays it cool and doesn't push, but the girls are concerned about Stacy and are excited to have an adult they can talk to and level with. They suggested Kathleen meet with Stacy. Kathleen agrees to accompany them and go down to the beach. The girls tell Kathleen she can pick up Stacy in Costa Mesa and they all piled into Kathleen's Volkswagen for the outing.

We figure letting Stacy know that her folks hired PIs to find her and how we did it could work against us if she runs away again. Our plan is to pick up Stacy and go to the beach. Then have the police pick her up when Kathleen drops her off. The Costa Mesa juvenile detectives are great and agreed to help us.

Kathleen spends the whole afternoon with Stacy and her friends who haven't seen her since she ran away. Her friends are both titillated and aghast to hear she had been living with a bunch of hippies who have been having sex with her and even passing her around.

When she left home, Stacy was wearing braces. Unlike today when retainers are a status symbol, at that time it was just one more thing her parents made her do that she hated. One of the hippies thought the braces made her look under-age and was afraid the police would bust him for contributing. So, he sat on her chest and removed the braces with a pair of pliers. She wanted them off, but admitted this was not a very pleasant experience.

The girls tried to talk Stacy into coming home because they were afraid something would happen to her. Kathleen tried to stay neutral. But Stacy was adamant about not going home. Costa Mesa PD allowed me to wait there for the call. Kathleen called me when they were leaving the beach as we planned. She told me where she would drop off Stacy on a main thoroughfare.

I drove to a spot near the proposed pickup spot accompanied by a Costa Mesa black and white which parked on the side street. When I see Kathleen's car approach, I give them the high sign. Stacy gets out, there are tearful goodbyes and Kathleen drives away with the girls. Stacy starts walking, apparently toward a house where she's now living with some new acquaintances she met after the hippies in the van kicked her out.

Waiting only a minute or two the two uniformed officers in the black-and-white cruise up and hail Stacy to come over to the car. They make it look routine and ask for ID. Then the officers radio in to make it look like they are just checking for warrants. The dispatcher advises them she's a runaway and to bring her in. It takes a couple of hours for Stacy's folks to get there. I sit in the background, as if I'm a police person while the female juvenile officer takes a statement from Stacy.

The parents pick her up and I can see she has mixed emotions about returning home. She didn't relish deprivation on the streets, but she wasn't happy at home either.

I instructed Kathleen to ease off a little from her subterfuge with Stacy and her friend's, but to keep it warm on the back burner. Neither Stacy nor the girls ever suspected they had been set up. Kathleen met with the girls, which now included Stacy on two more occasions. She established a solid rapport with Stacy, who would call her a couple times a week to talk. As we had feared about a month later Stacy called Kathleen to say she was going to run away again. She did. Only this time we helped. But this story has a great ending.

After Stacy came home the second time the parents got her into school for troubled kids. She did great and became a solid citizen. She became a registered nurse and at the last report had her own family. She still doesn't know Kathleen's true occupation or any details of what we did. But it worked!

A MYSTERY HOMICIDE

A big Los Angeles law firm calls with a special job which they want me to handle personally. Their client is a Japanese publication.

A Japanese woman, married to a Japanese man, and living in the San Gabriel Valley is murdered. Our law firm client's client, a respected Japanese magazine, has printed a story by a Japanese reporter which suggests that the husband is suspected of the murder by the police. The husband is suing for libel.

Running down the possible sources of this statement was very complicated. It involved the interviews of several detectives of a San Gabriel Valley police department including the Chief of Police. The police were very guarded in their statements and obviously didn't wish to get dragged into a law suit. But the most interesting interview to me was that of the county coroner.

In preparation for the interview, I did a little search on the Internet of this famous fellow whose nick name is "Coroner to the Stars." The problem of course is you have to separate the facts from the hyperbole. I did the best I could though I was already aware of some of the controversy surrounding the coroner's background.

Thomas T. Noguchi was appointed Chief Medical Examiner-Coroner for Los Angeles County in 1961. When he performed Marilyn Monroe's autopsy in 1962 his profile raised considerably. Subsequently, he also autopsied many other movie stars including Manson murder victim Sharon Tate.

Some controversy arose following his autopsy of Senator Robert Kennedy. Noguchi found that Sirhan Sirhan's murder weapon was very close to Kennedy's right ear when he fired into the back of the Senator's head, while other witnesses claimed Sirhan was at least three feet away. This resulted in speculation that there was more than one shooter.

Noguchi's findings regarding the cause of death of actress Natalie Wood, have also been questioned. But I digress . . .

When I interviewed Coroner Noguchi he was friendly but also seemed to be on his guard. I wondered if he had been the one to tell the police that he suspected the husband was guilty of the homicide in the case. Mr. Noguchi obviously didn't want to speculate for the record, but finally said, "If I had to pick someone, it would be the husband." I think the only reason Mr. Noguchi remembered this older case was because the victim and the husband were of Japanese descent. He repeatedly denied speaking to a reporter

As often happens in these cases, after our negative findings were relayed to the Japanese client, we heard nothing further. But meeting and discussing the case with the "Coroner to the Stars" was quite interesting.

JAVA JAVA

or

Maybe Crime Really Does Pay

Remember the old Ink Spots tune from the 40s called Java Java? You don't? How old are you anyway? Geez!

One of the fun things we get to do in the office (the field investigators have the real fun) is to think up code names for sensitive files. I started this back in the early 60s when we all partied pretty hard and got a big job from a utility company. So that nobody would be compromised by mentioning the client's name in a saloon, we called it the HUSH case. But that's another story.

Java Java was an interesting case, although ultimately very frustrating. I hate to see the bad guy win.

This job involved the mellifluous names that you see on TV and associate with aroma, relaxation, satisfaction, and even sex. Names like Maxwell House, Folgers, Yuban, Tasters Choice and my favorite . . . Kona.

The president of the coffee company was a smooth Irishman I'll call Dugan. His lawyer told him I could help. A consummate salesman, as soon as he had spilled his tale of woe and asked what it would cost, the second question out of his mouth was "what coffee service was I using" and "why was I not using his service?"

These are the guys who supply all the coffee, hot chocolate, soups, etc. to offices big and small. Dugan said his Big Time Coffee company was the largest in Los Angeles and modestly admitted it was the best too.

Coffee is usually pretty expensive and a salable commodity at all times with a ready black-market. Dugan showed me his operation which seemed pretty foolproof. At the back of the warehouse there are a series of padlocked cages. During the day the warehouse staff calculates the orders for each driver and places the packaged coffee to be delivered the following day in each drivers padlocked cage. The drivers arrive early the next morning before the company opens. They access the main warehouse door, then unlock their own padlock and empty the cases of coffee from their cage into their delivery truck. When they open the warehouse door, their alarm codes are recorded with an opening and closing time.

Dugan said he had had some inventory shortages in the past and one driver had lost a whole truckload to a robbery. But right now, he was not aware of any substantial shrinkage. So, "What's the problem?" I asked. He said his largest competitor in the business had told Dugan that his Big Time Coffee might have an employee theft problem. I regarded that suspiciously, but Dugan assured me the competitors are good people. When I met and worked with them, it proved to be true. In fact, they really stuck their neck out for a competitor just to correct a wrong.

It seems the other coffee company, who I'll call Hills Brothers, were making a delivery into a high-rise downtown. Youngest brother, Rich Hills, was the deliveryman. The building security guard offered to sell him coffee in quantity and for half what they pay wholesale. Hills reported this to his brother the president.

The first offer had been nine months before, but since that time, the guard kept pestering him. This guard was a real entrepreneur. He was selling fresh eggs, vegetables, and even bread to people in the building. Hills said he knew that Dugan supplied coffee to the bulk of customers in the building and suspected that one of Dugan's drivers was supplying the guard. But when Hills asked the guard about his source of supply, the guard was evasive saying he got the coffee from a Chinaman.

I set up a meeting with the Hills Brothers and asked them to show some interest in the guard's offer and see if they could place an order. After all, we had nothing to lose because the guard was selling coffee for less than our costs. When Hills told the guard he would like to place an order for 30 cases of Yuban, the guard said he would call to make the arrangements. Hills followed the guard back to his cubicle where the guard looked up at a sheet of paper pasted on the wall which had a bunch of phone numbers. As the guard moved his finger over the paper, Rich Hills saw the area of the paper where the guard was pointing as he phoned. The guard said there was no answer, but he would make the call later.

The next day, Hills came by the building and the guard was busy at the other end of the loading dock. Hills slipped into the guard cubicle and scanned the sheet of paper with the phone numbers on it. He tried to memorize the numbers he was looking at and note the name alongside of it. Back out on the dock, he acted like he had been looking for the guard. The guard said he could pick up the coffee in three days. Hills phoned me to say he was not positive he had the phone number right but the name next to it was Pete.

At the Big Time Coffee company Dugan gave me a list of the drivers, their addresses and phone numbers. One of them was Pete Lomoco and his number was very close to what Hills had seen posted in the guard shack. When Dugan saw this, he began to curse. "Lomoco is the s.o.b. who claimed he was robbed and lost a whole truck load of Yuban!"

I told Dugan I did not want to alert any of his people in case Lomoco had an inside man, but I needed someone to give me a hand after hours. He introduced me to his vice president who I will call Gruesome, because that rhymes with his name. He was not really Gruesome, but his face showed the ravages of drinking something stronger than coffee and chain smoking. His complexion was florid and his bulbous nose had pores that looked like craters on the moon. He was a drunk with an expense account whose job it was to entertain other drunks. Sound familiar?

I made arrangements to meet Gruesome at the coffee company at midnight. As I was following Gruesome into the warehouse he turned to speak and the alcohol on his breath nearly blew me over. I guess he needed a lot of fortification to stay up so late. We opened Lomoco's cage from the inside and saw it was loaded with the next day's orders. That night, I marked every case with an ultraviolet crayon, invisible to the naked eye. I came back with Gruesome several more times and repeated the process. Each night the marking included the date and my initials.

After the three-day wait, Rich Hills went to the high-rise but the guard was suspicious. He asked Hills to pay him in advance so Rich gave him half the money. The guard told him to come back in an hour. When Hills returned, 12 cases of Yuban were on the loading dock. The guard said he would have the rest in two days. Hills took delivery and paid him the balance in cash.

When we wheeled the coffee into my office and turned on the ultraviolent light, I was surprised to find only one case of the 12 had my initials and date in the ultraviolet crayon. When I told Dugan, he said, "The bastard's got his own inventory to sell from." We would like to have seen the inside of the Lomoco's garage, but during our surveillance he was always very careful about keeping the door closed.

Finally, one of our guys got a glimpse before Lomoco closed the door. He said there were a bunch of boxes of something in one corner of the garage that could be cases of coffee.

Meanwhile Rich Hills picked up the rest of his order and placed additional orders. My office was beginning to look like a Jamaican warehouse. The second batch of 10 cases all had our mark and date. The next two groups only had one and two cases respectively without my mark. We seem to have reached the point of diminishing return.

I had Rich Hills execute a declaration and I prepared my own along with the final reports. Later I picked up Gruesome and took the paperwork to LAPD's Southwest station to file the complaint. The trick is to get them interested so they don't brush us off.

I have a friend who was a Hollywood PD narcotics lieutenant. He told me that they are lucky if they have time to handle 10% of the leads they get from citizens and other sources. Imagine having a business where there is always more work than you can handle. Once they get into the case, of course, they do what they have to do and they often have to work after hours. But the brass is always trying to limit over-time or accrued time off which is usually the case.

So Gruesome and I are ushered into the back room which has bilious green walls kind of like the gas chamber at San Quentin. The detective in his shirt-sleeves replete with hip holster (only the yuppy cops wear shoulder rigs like in the movies) looks up and seems to gather a pained expression when it appears all others in the room are going to ignore us. He is obliged to ask what we want because we made eye contact. They all look up though when they hear I'm a private eye. I can immediately sense judgments being made.

At least half the cops think PIs are jerks. Most have never met one but their sergeant told them this in training. The sergeant probably got his opinion from watching Boston Blackie make a monkey out of Inspector Faraday.

I always go out of my way to be polite and professional with them no matter how off-putting their behavior. Invariably I get the cop interested in what we are doing and then the whole bunch of them give us a lot of assistance. This detective looked like he was getting an Excedrin headache as I tried to explain the crime we thought was taking place. It went something like this:

"You say someone is stealing Mr. Gruesome's coffee and selling it for half its wholesale, cost?

Yes.

But you say except for the truck hijacking, none of your coffee is missing.

Yes.

Then where pray tell is the stolen coffee coming from?

We think it is being skimmed from our customer's orders.

Then why don't you get them to come down here and sign the complaint.

We can't do that because they are not aware of the fact that they have been robbed of the coffee. It would be worse than awkward for us to tell them that we think the employee may have been ripping them off for some time."

I explained how much coffee would be used by a law firm with 300 lawyers and 600 support staff occupying 10 floors with a kitchen on each floor. How easy it would be to short the order a few pounds or even a full case when you observe the customer didn't count it carefully.

The detective was sympathetic. He took the complaint and agreed to help us arrest the bad guys with the goods when we made our last buy. The next day they were with us when we staked out the high-rise. Pete Lomoco made his delivery and the cops followed him away and arrested him out of sight of the building. Hills made the buy from the guard and paid him with marked money. The cops arrested him and a black-and-white took him in after we advised the building staff they needed to cover the guard station. I took the last batch of coffee back to my office and the police booked the marked money.

I thought we had a pretty good case. I was wrong.

One of the most frustrating aspects of criminal cases is the time wasted going to trials that are continued and the hours you spend in the hallway waiting for your case to be called. This process discourages business people from pressing criminal charges because of the lost time and the cost of paying your employees to stand in the hall is significant. But of course, this is what the defense lawyers count on. Delay, delay, delay . . . deny, deny, deny. Usually the evidence gets weaker, the witness recollections get hazier and many times evidence is lost.

But Pete Lomoco's case was only continued once following the arraignment and we shortly found ourselves in the hallway of Municipal Court once again. You have to present your initial case in Municipal Court. Then the judge decides if the defendant will be bound over for trial in Superior Court. Rich Hills was pacing up and down silently cursing himself for ever getting involved and looking uncomfortable in a suit and tie. Dugan was grumbling about the wait as if it were my fault and Gruesome looked like he needed a drink.

Our case was finally called. The DA put Dugan on the stand to establish the loss. I was surprised the coffee salesman didn't ask the judge what coffee service they were using in the courthouse. Dugan testified that he didn't have an inventory loss. The judge dutifully listened to Hills and me and received our evidence. The defense lawyer moved to dismiss on the grounds that there was no theft because we did not have a victim who could prove a loss.

The judge told Pete to stand up. She said, "I know what you've been doing Mr. Lomoco and I wish that I could do something about it, but unfortunately your victims are not in court today. Case dismissed."

We trooped out like pallbearers after a wake. Pete Lomoco gave us a wise ass grin. The DA wished the cops hadn't talked him into filing the case. Dugan and Gruesome looked at me like I had stolen the coffee. I called their lawyer Sly, who had referred them to me. He understood and told me it wasn't my fault and we commiserated that at least Pete got fired so he wouldn't steal from Dugan again. That's what we thought.

Two weeks later it was Sly on the phone again. Pete had filed for unemployment and the State didn't accept Dugan's explanation that Lomoco had been fired for cause. They wanted a hearing. As often happens in these hearings, the Administrative Law Judge takes the part of the fired employee and puts the employer and their witnesses on trial. A surprising number of AL judges are ex-union business agents which probably explains it.

This hearing rang true to form. Gruesome and I told our story. Pete Lomoco testified that he was being persecuted by Dugan and his thugs and he had already been found not guilty by the Municipal Judge. I tried to point out that that was not quite true and in fact the case was only dismissed on a technicality. The Administrative Law Judge thought Pete Lomoco was a hell of a lot better guy than Gruesome and me and he granted benefits to Pete retroactively.

I phoned Dugan to tell them we lost round two. He said he would let me know if they wanted to appeal, but the way the case had gone, he was not surprised.

He *was* surprised a few days later when we he was served with a civil suit charging malicious prosecution, wrongful infliction of emotional distress, invasion of privacy and a couple of other things I can't remember. My company and I were named as additional defendants.

Pete's lawyer was a jerk from Leimert Park. On the day of my deposition, his lawyer couldn't be there so he gave it to his partner who was also a jerk, but a dumb one. The lawyer from my insurance company was Tom Tellall who was top drawer. The substitute didn't know what questions to ask. We killed them in the deposition and later got the case dismissed.

We buy our coffee from Dugan so I guess we worked out what he paid us for the investigation. Gruesome's liver gave out to cirrhosis and killed him before his lung cancer got the chance to do the job. I ran up against my lawyer Tom Tellall the other day when I had a rare role as witness for the plaintiff. He wouldn't stop grinning during the cross-examination and he really took it easy on me, but he won a defense verdict.

This happened a few years ago. Today, Pete Lomoco would have also filed a fraudulent Worker's Compensation claim for stress and after drawing substantial temporary disability while moonlighting or thieving would probably settle for 50 grand or more. For all I know, he may even be in jail today. If he isn't, you can bet he's stealing from somebody and probably getting away with it.

MANY THNGS BEGIN AT THE AIRPORT

As I write this, it is sixty-one years since my first job that involved LAX. That place has changed substantially since I did my first work there in 1960. Then, the airport was essentially one building and we could send one operative to cover all incoming and outgoing flights. Flying costs a lot more than the train or the Greyhound bus which was all my family could afford. In 1960, absent a family emergency, most people who flew were either well off or famous, or both. I often saw movie stars.

My first day there, Tarzan, (Johnny Weissmuller) stood out, as did actors Linda Darnell and Gene Kelly who walked like he had springs under his shoes and carried an infectious grin. But my most memorable celebrity was even more famous.

There was no security or gates even in those days, and you could walk out onto the tarmac unimpeded. In between the flights I was to cover, I wandered out one door to see what was happening.

An international flight was just unloading. I saw a lady carrying a bag that looked like it was made of carpet, starting toward the terminal. It was former first lady Eleanor Roosevelt. Nobody with her. I met her halfway and offered to carry her bag into the terminal. A young man who looked embarrassed to be late, rushed to meet her and took the bag. She graciously thanked me for assisting her. Mrs. Roosevelt passed away nearly two years later on November 7, 1962, and thanks to FDR's fourth term, she still holds the record as the longest serving first lady. But I digress . . .

Placing people under surveillance when they arrive at LAX is a nerve-racking assignment, particularly because you usually don't know what mode of transportation they will use. Currently, I would suggest no less than three operatives and communications are essential. Before cell phones, things were different. One of my best pieces of luck happened in 1964, when we were very busy with the HUSH case and a lot of other assignments.

Thanks to a request from my assistant manager Bob Morris, an amateur actor, I had hired the husband of one of Bob's co-actors. Jim Haggin was a story in himself. He was the great-grandson of James Ben Ali Haggin who is sometimes referred to as "the father of thoroughbred racing in America". A Wikipedia story in itself.

While juggling a myriad of cases we received a domestic relations assignment that a New York law firm had relayed to a big firm in Los Angeles. Other than his name and the fact he was tall and had a prominent nose, the only other identifying information on our work sheet was that he had Gucci luggage. Since all of our operatives were busy, I decided to work the case myself and asked Jim Haggin to assist me.

I had a bad habit of timing plane arrival for national flights like most of the ones we met which were from San Francisco.

So Haggin and I were enjoying a dinner of bacon wrapped shrimp at the Coachman in Pasadena when I realized we were about to miss the New York arrival. We got in my Mustang and set some new records from Pasadena to LAX.

At the curb outside "LUGGAGE" we parked behind another Mustang and bolted into the arrival area. Unfortunately, the flight had already arrived and the luggage was coming down the conveyor. A tall guy with a prominent nose was nowhere to be seen. So, I looked at the work sheet again and asked Haggin, "What the hell is <u>Gucci</u> luggage?" Jim reached into his pocket and pulled out his key chain which I had noticed before and consisted of a red and green canvas fabric fob with a stirrup to hold the keys. He said the bags would have the distinctive red and green fabric.

At that moment, I spied the red and green decorated bags coming down the conveyor. When the sky cap loaded up the luggage on a cart and swung by a couple seated on the wall, we realized where the tall, prominent nose was. The skycap wheeled the luggage out to the curb and loaded it into the Mustang in front of our car. Pretty easy tail so far.

Driving away from the terminal, they headed down Sepulveda and took Lincoln to the California Incline which led to the Pacific Coast Highway that paralleled the beach. Passing Topanga Canyon, they soon passed the Sea Lion restaurant in Malibu, then slowed as if looking for an address. Shortly they made a U-turn and soon did another. Finally, they pulled into a driveway and he carried his luggage inside a two-story Malibu beach house of considerable size. In today's dollars, while the home wasn't in the "colo-ny", I'm sure it is worth more than ten million.

We were in suits. I changed to my painting coveralls, Haggin took off his jacket. When we got down on the beach, we could barely see over the bulkhead into the living room. As we did, we were just in time to see the front door closing. The couple left without us, but we caught up with them as they walked from their car in the parking lot to the Sea Lion. I quickly put my suit back on.

The Sea Lion has a row of individually divided, two-seat, private booths looking out over the flood lighted, crashing surf. It can be very romantic, but I wondered if Haggin and I should hold hands to not look out of place. Fortunately, we found a seat at the nearby bar where we could see our subjects coming or going. They apparently stayed for two drinks, then went back to the house. I got back into my coveralls, clambered onto the beach and observed that the downstairs lights were out and shortly, the upstairs lights too. We left.

The next day, I sent Haggin downtown to run the property records for the beach house. Then we realized why the lady had trouble locating the home. It was probably because she had so many.

Since she is still living, I won't reveal her identity. Her family is nationally known and extremely wealthy New Yorkers. The gentleman, who is now deceased was a former member of the OSS which became the CIA. He was a much-decorated war hero and who had held many important and famous positions in his life.

We forwarded the results of our surveillance to New York and were advised no further surveillance was necessary.

Sadly, my wingman, Jim Haggin, was killed a few years ago when he fell off his polo pony in the Santa Barbara area and was kicked in the head.

THE RETURN OF THE DESERT RAT

A long story, but it all ties together:

After I convinced USO Junior Hostess Marcia Bankhead to be my bride, I needed to find a place for us to live at Ft. Campbell, Kentucky. There weren't very many possibilities, but there were a few trailer parks. My Dad loaned me some money and in Nashville, I bought a new 33' x 8' house trailer and parked it outside the gate a half mile or so. Later, I rented a space on the base from the Department of the Army for $8.33 per month. This included sewer, electric and water, plus weekly trash pick-up by the stockade prisoners, but just a gravel patio.

When I got ready for discharge in 1955, I asked my Dad (Irv) to find me a trailer park in the Los Angeles area where we could park it. The Army rules are that when you honorably leave the service, they will pay your transportation back to the place where you enlisted and amazingly, this included transporting your trailer at no charge. This, after they had been paying me $300 per month cash as a staff sergeant for parachuting out of perfectly good airplanes. Best job I ever had, at that point.

But when Irv told the trailer parks we had a child, he found that most were adults only, even though our kid was only two months. So, he got interested in trailer parks and bought one in Inglewood, California. Later, he bought another in

Norwalk which Marcia managed for five years. They were successful businesses.

In 1962, the same salesman sold him a lease on 26 acres in Indian Springs, Nevada, 45 miles northwest of Las Vegas and sixteen miles from the Nevada Test Site. Irv had decided to build a modern mobile home park that would accommodate the latest models. Accompanied by my two young brothers, Gary and Richard, they commenced construction, which required a great deal of concrete for pads and curbs. When the Las Vegas concrete outfits created problems, Irv bought his own portable batch plant, two used ready-mix trucks, and became a Kaiser Permanente dealer. My brother Gary sold concrete all over town besides mixing what we needed for the Mobile Home Park. This went well until there was a strike at the Test Site. Suddenly we were crawling with union business agents. We were asked (really told) to join Local 5. When we declined, the Union guys informed us they would set up an "informational" picket line around our batch plant to prevent Kaiser Permanente's union drivers from delivering cement to our plant. Although Irv mentioned we needed back-fill for some of our empty ditches, he finally gave in and Gary joined Local 5.

Meanwhile, I had been working as an investigator for Krout & Schneider since January, 1960. Things in the Springs weren't going too well. So, in May of 1963 I took a leave of absence from K & S and with my camera, my little family moved to Indian Springs, Nevada, to help with building the park. I was there one year to the day. Keeping my relationship with K & S going, I had applied for a detective license for K & S in Nevada. I also applied for the lead investigative job at the test site working for the general contractor, Reynolds Electric. This job paid $1,200 per month and I was #1 on their waiting list.

Now it was May 1964 and we were just pouring the swimming pool concrete. Our schedule since 1963 had been to work six and one-half days per week, usually 12-hour days . . . or longer. We took Sunday afternoons off. Bags of cement weigh 94 pounds each. So, on this May evening, after dinner, a shower, and two Tom Collins, I was bushed and climbing into bed when the phone rang. It was Marvin Stevens, our best op in the L.A. office.

Marv had a little Hillman convertible. He said he was tailing two guys in a big Buick wagon who had stopped for gas in Victorville and figured they were headed for Las Vegas. Marv said he probably wouldn't be able to stay up with their speed and asked if I could go to Vegas and head them off. Marvin said that he knew I was 45 miles northwest of Vegas and Victorville was 144 miles south, so I had plenty of time to get there. Remember, these were the days before cell phones. Marv would stop at a pay phone, and call Marcia after he arrived to find where the pair ended up. My adrenalin started pumping, tired as I was. I gassed up my Rambler wagon and was quickly Vegas bound.

If the reader has been to Las Vegas lately, you know that I-15 consists of five or six lanes of heavy traffic on either side. But in pre-Howard Hughes 1964 Vegas, I-15 was a two-lane road with a ditch on the side and the Strip ended at Tropicana. I pulled my wheels across the ditch just South of that and waited for a big Buick with a whip-antennae. I made them immediately and tailed them to the Sawdust (which is what the locals called the Stardust). I phoned Marcia to let her know they had checked in at the Stardust. Marv arrived a few minutes later, after calling Marcia and met me at the hotel. I was glad to be relieved, tired as I was. But that feeling of relief passed when Marvin informed me that he had a hearing in L.A. the next day and had to fly back tonight. He informed me this was an important surveillance on a big new job we were doing for Pacific Bell. Somehow, I stayed awake until his return the following afternoon. We watched them for five days as they appeared to be installing something electronic.

This was the beginning of the biggest investigation in our company history. We modified what had been called "the phone company" job, to the code name the "Hush Case".

The details of this case are outlined in the following chapter. It lasted almost two years and resulted in substantial growth of our Los Angeles office.

After five days and nights in Vegas, I felt like I was back in the saddle and not enthused about returning to construc-tion. I called the L.A. Manager, Maurice "Truck" Hannah, and asked if he needed any help. He said he did and since he was going on vacation, asked if I would return and run the office in his absence. A month later, for reasons I won't go into, the home office assigned me to manage the office per-manently. I remember those days in Indian Springs fondly, but I never looked back.

THE "HUSH" CASE

This was the largest single investigation ever conducted by Krout & Schneider involved thousands of hours of work over 18 months in the Los Angeles area, beginning in 1964. We code-named the case "HUSH" and admonished our operatives to stop referring to the case as the "phone" case, when they were talking shop at the end of the day

The Bell Laboratories had just invented the system which allowed for long distance calls to be made and automatically charged to phone bills by merely dialing "1" before the number instead of having to go through a long-distance operator. The investment made by AT&T to change the country's whole system was a substantial part of the company's net worth.

The expert engineers didn't reckon with dishonest entrepreneurs figuring out a way to outsmart the new billing system. A handful of electronic sharpies soon devised a means of circumventing the charge part of the new system. For as little as $25 to $40, the crooks could go to the equivalent of Radio Shack and purchase components to create a cigar box sized device. On any telephone, they could connect two wires to the gadget and dial long distance anywhere in the world, free of charge.

Also unfortunately, existing law did not make it a crime to do so. The crooks even appeared on Walter Cronkite's program to brag about their devices which they were selling for $750 to $1,000.

While telephone company lobbyists set to work to try to get new laws enacted in Sacramento and Washington, Pacific Telephone Special Agents, using Krout & Schneider, set about gathering evidence.

There was more than one set of crooks making and selling these devices. The K & S investigation involved extensive surveillance of multiple parties and a very elaborate sting by our operative Jim Haggin posing as a photo journalist.

To establish Haggin's cover, we needed to create a record that the bad guys couldn't penetrate. We obtained a social security card and a drivers license. At the credit bureau which was in the Subway Terminal Building on Hope Street we visited the red-haired lady named Sally who ran the place. Sally did us favors from time to time and we gave her a bottle at Christmas time.

The credit bureau records consisted of a massive number of file cabinets in one huge room. Sally located the file cabinet with the name we were creating, all in alphabetical order. In the proper drawer and file, I was able to have her place a card with the personal information like all the other records. It worked well because we applied for a Diner's Club card and it was received in short order.

Using his journalist subterfuge, Haggin was able to gain lawful entry to the businesses and establish a rapport with the crooks who were manufacturing the devices. He obtained undercover films and sound recordings, to be used as evidence. Believe it or not, at that time we were using Minox miniature cameras and wire recorders. But I'm dating myself.

In the meantime, statutes were enacted in Sacramento and Washington to make the manufacture and sale of these devices unlawful, which shut down the problem.

ADDING K & S SECURITY

Our company had been solely an investigation agency since 1927, unlike others such as Pinkerton which became primarily a guard company. In 1972, President Al Moffat and I wondered if we were missing something. Moffat applied for a Private Patrol Operator's license and started a patrol in Marin County and providing guard service in Downtown San Francisco.

My opinion of many guard companies and their employees, was not very high. I wanted to provide a better-quality service. I alerted some law firm clients that we were offering a higher caliber officer and that we could provide security for strikes. There seemed to be many strikes at the time. We offered our applicants substantially higher pay and advertised we were looking for military veterans.

U.S. BORAX STRIKE

In early June, 1974, I received a call from a labor lawyer asking if I could provide a dozen "super guards" (his words not mine) for a pending strike in the desert at the U.S. Borax Company. He explained that his client at Boron in the Mojave Desert, had already employed the services of two Kern County guard companies to guard the main factory complex, but that they were concerned about possible vandalism at key water wells located about two miles away.

Our security manager was Larry Kimmel who had recently been discharged from the Green Berets and served as a Captain in Viet Nam. Kimmel and eleven officers were sent to Boron on what was the eve of the contract expiration. They were equipped with heavy-duty flak vests and steel Kel-Lite flashlights. The client had explained they would feed our officers.

At 7 AM the next morning my home phone rang. Kimmel said "Boss, you're not going to believe this, but we had a riot here last night and several buildings were burned. The client radioed me to leave the water wells and come to the complex." He said Borax had issued axe handles to their management personnel and was glad that we had our Kel-Lites. He said some of the Kern County Sheriffs may have retreated as had some officers of the other two guard companies allegedly due to having relatives in the striker's ranks. Apparently, several hundred striking employees had gathered outside the gates to join the swing shift workers who were coming off-shift. These employees were members of the I.L.W.U., the longshoreman's union. Years before the Borax employees were represented by the AFL/CIO but eventually switched to the more militant I.L.W.U.

The next day, our labor lawyer client advised that Borax intended to dismiss the other two guard companies and asked if we could handle the whole job. Later, we also were asked to handle the Borax facility in the harbor at Wilmington where the company had another facility. The strike lasted 132 days.

According to a lengthy article published in the December 1974 issue of Fortune Magazine titled *"HOW THE TENDERFEET TOUGHENED UP U.S. BORAX"* the Longshoremen's union had continued to increase demands for not only higher pay, but more control of what the Borax management could do. Borax was planning to do some construction and the I.L.W.U. wanted to choose the construction company. This was the last straw and Borax management decided they would take a strike, if necessary. Management was also concerned about the dwindling production of Borax which was in high demand and the Boron plant produced 60% of the world supply.

Borax decided, if necessary, to operate the Boron and smaller Wilmington plant, with supervisory and salaried personnel. They called for volunteers of non-union employees from all over the company. The normal Boron workforce is over 1,400. Management considered at best they would have 450 volunteers. These included managers, secretaries, clerks, salesmen, computer specialists, engineers and scientific researchers.

Once you get a borax refinery in operation, you have to keep it going 24 hours per day. The basic refining process consists mainly of dumping crushed ore into hot water which extracts the soluble borax from the insoluble clay and then pipes the solution to multiple parts of the plant to be turned into various borax products. The plant had to be operated 24 hours per day since the borax was heated and had to be kept moving or it would harden in the pipes.

The volunteers assembled in Los Angeles and were flown to the company's Mojave-desert air strip. Some were no doubt shocked by the barren landscape, the desert heat and the 80-acre plant covered in white dust.

In the days before the expiration of the union contract, worker intransigence increased as did sabotage such as plastic baggies in gas tanks of earth movers and trucks.

The company hired caterers who normally provided food for motion picture crews. The Borax "scabs" ate well including often on steak and lobster. K & S Security increased its ranks as the other two guard companies' employees departed. We recruited many returning Viet Nam vets who were accustomed to heat and depravation. Twice a week, on Wednesdays and Saturdays, Borax issued two cans of beer per employee.

Soon, production began to increase. The volunteers worked 12-hour days for eighteen days straight before being allowed four days to go home. Esprit de corps was high among this crew. Not only did production greatly increase, but the "scabs" cleaned up the piles of Borax dust which were waste high and had accumulated over the years.

Meanwhile, violence occurred in the nearby town of Boron and many families were torn by different loyalties. Some families had three generations who had worked in the plant. Family members who crossed the picket lines clashed with those who were honoring the picket lines.

At the gates and picket lines, we were constantly dealing with violence and vandalism of entering vehicles. Although our officers were instructed not to speak to the picketers or antagonize them, mayhem was sometimes unavoidable.

In September, Borax sent a letter to the striking employees advising that the company would begin hiring permanent replacements to fill the jobs of employees who were not back at work by September 23, 1974. Two dozen strikers returned to work in spite of threats and violence by the strikers. On the morning of September 23, strikers lined the roads to the plant, stoning every car going in or out and injuring several people.

Things got tougher for our officers too. But what really hurt the Longshoreman Union's situation was when members of the AFL/CIO who had projects to man in the plant, refused to honor the I.L.W.U picket lines. The replacement workers who mostly lived in nearby communities like Barstow,

Mojave and Lancaster gathered every morning and evening to form 100-car convoys to the plant and were escorted by police cars headed by a helicopter.

The union met on October 7 and voted to reject the most recent Borax offer. As a result, hiring of replacements increased. At least 250 new workers had been hired by the time the union met again on October 24 and voted to end the strike and come back to work.

At K & S Security, we were kept busy supplying staff and dealing with a few problems such as when two of our guards rolled over a rented truck driving recklessly in the desert. Thanks to the seat belts, they were not injured. Unfortunately, I ended up having to buy the damaged truck, but that's another story.

This job proved that K & S Security could handle tough challenges which it did for ten more years as strikes tapered off and were very infrequent.

HOLLYWOOD PARK RACE TRACK

The two largest race tracks in the Los Angeles area were Santa Anita in Arcadia and Hollywood Park in Inglewood. Over the years, management had usually caved in when threatened with a strike, whether on pay or sometimes, for benefits. But in 1979, the pari-mutual clerks at Hollywood Park were concerned that a new computer system might threaten their jobs. Famously tough negotiator, owner Marjorie Everett was not intimidated by the union and K & S Security was called in to help keep the track running. We handled many positions besides back track security and did ticket taking, program sales to name a few.

Fortunately, Santa Anita loaned Hollywood Park their General Manager who helped us neophytes learn and get the job done. When a race would go off, everyone in the crowd was looking at the horses and the track. I was always looking the other way, watching for malfeasance by my employees. Race track patrons are mainly of a similar breed and would rather toke a guard than paying the track the same amount for a pass.

The Horse Racing Board held a hearing at the track chaired by the recently appointed Governor's Chief of Staff Gray Davis. I was standing next to jockey Willie Shoemaker. When the politicians stated that Hollywood Park was violating personal safety by having un-trained people staffing the park, Willie muttered an expletive saying that Davis's statements were B.S. You may recall that Gray Davis later became Governor but was voted out of office. But that's another story.

The strike only lasted 30 days, but learning how a race track operates was the experience of a lifetime for me. It was sad to see the entire complex demolished and it's amazing to see the multi-billion-dollar SoFi Stadium and some housing arise in its place. The 70,000-seat stadium now is the site of both the L.A. Rams and L.A. Chargers football games and is scheduled for a Super Bowl.

MAYNARD HUMMEL NEEDS A JOB

Many years after I had left American Service Bureau and was with Krout & Schneider, we were living on Mount Olympus. One morning, I got a call from my former boss Maynard Hummel asking to see me. It was raining when he arrived at my house. He seemed to have fear in his eyes. He was now retired but his pension was not enough to get by on. He was approaching 70 and needed a job, but no one would hire him because of his age.

Our best client was the largest law firm in Los Angeles, O'Melveny and Myers. In addition to doing their investigative work, and strikes for their labor lawyers' clients, K & S Security also provided security guards in their high-rise office. I made Hummel a lieutenant and put him in charge of the account. He loved it.

Every day, every lawyer passing his desk at the entrance called him by his first name which made him feel good. The U.S. Secretary of State, Warren Christopher was a partner in the firm and Hummel was proud when Mr. Christopher would arrive and say "Good morning, Maynard." Hummel continued working for us for several years and now survived into his second retirement quite nicely.

I never held it against Hummel for firing me at the behest of a dumb vice president from Chicago at ASB.

DECATUR

I have always felt a little silly saying, "You're under arrest." I've never been a copper. People always ask me.

I am a real detective, but I seldom carry a gun and never carry handcuffs. I only weigh 180 and my ex-paratrooper nose has been broken enough - thank you. So, in the back of my mind, a little voice is saying, "What if he resists?" Or worse yet, "What if he ignores me?" Then what do I do? Knock him down? After all, a private eye is just a citizen, not a peace officer. And the civil liability for false arrest and all the paper work that goes with it can break you.

The following is a true story that occurred in the late '60s prior to cell phones:

I was the thirty-four-year-old Los Angeles branch manager of a large San Francisco-headquartered detective agency. We were running a dozen insurance fraud surveillances per day and had another six or seven investigators doing a variety of things. I had two good supervisors running the surveillance crew, and a cracker jack named Maria, honchoing the investigations.

Agency policy dictated we always get the money up front unless the client was gold plated, and sometimes, even then. I got lazy and wasn't paying attention like a manager should, when the boss called to ask about a file that Maria had been handling. It seems we had a substantial initial retainer, but no subsequent bills had been paid and there was work completed but unbilled. He chewed harder, when it was obvious, I was not on top of it. If Maria had a fault, it was getting too personally involved with some of the cases.

Our client was a wealthy and influential Kern County oil man whose grandchildren were allegedly abducted by his daughter's ex-husband. I say allegedly, because I initially suspected the client had used his influence to get a Kern County judge to issue a felony warrant for child stealing, a rarity in those days. His daughter had legal custody, but the suspect was the natural father of the children.

It turns out the ex-son-in-law was a bad guy. He was a con man and apparent dope runner. He came to visit, then abducted his seven-year-old daughter and five-year old son. His unlikely moniker was Decatur Holcomb.

As I soon found out, Maria had traced Decatur to New York, and when our correspondent agency and NYPD got the landlord to open the door, there was a smoldering cigarette in the ash tray, but Decatur and the kids were gone. Maria got a lead that he was in Acapulco, and once again, we barely missed him as he incredibly escaped with the children. So, we had to lay out the cash to the agencies in New York and Mexico, but our client was taking the position he would not pay until he saw some results. It worked for him in Bakersfield, and it was working with us. We were upside down in this case - - Big Time!

Maria was in tight with the coppers at LAPD Intelligence (now Internal Affairs) and they were giving her some help, although the hot shot captain in charge, one Daryl Gates, was probably not aware of it. Maria learned that Decatur was in Los Angeles and had rented a car at the airport. She asked all of our troops to be on the lookout for the car, Decatur and the kids. That was our equivalent of putting out an all-points bulletin. With the size of Los Angeles, we were looking for the proverbial needle-in-a-hay stack. But like me, Maria is lucky.

Betty, a sharp investigator who both worked for Maria and made contacts for our surveillance operatives, was serving a subpoena in the Mid-Wilshire area when she spotted Decatur's rental car on the boulevard. She sprinted to a pay phone to tell Maria, then saw Decatur and the kids return to the car before help arrived.

Tailing in L.A. is a fine art. It takes a pro to follow someone without getting picked or losing them. As our longest running surveillance man once said, "It's not how many times you lose 'em, but how fast you find 'em again." You have to be aggressive but getting a ticket or in an accident, defeats the purpose. Betty got Decatur to the Sunset Strip, where Crescent Heights turns into Laurel Canyon, and lost him. She thought he might have turned North up the canyon.

We had no authorization to "throw out the drag net", as Jack Benny used to say, so Maria and I appealed to our troops for volunteers. Our idea was to blanket the area for an evening after work with as many cars as possible and hope we could spot Decatur. The operatives would receive no pay or mileage. Our esprit de corps was high. The first night we fielded eleven cars and got blanked. The next night we had thirteen cars, some with two people in them.

The only two-way radios we had were a few citizen band units which worked poorly, and not at all in Laurel Canyon. Our plan was to use the answering service as a communications center with everyone checking in every hour or so. Those with CB's would communicate as best they could. We fanned out, mostly cruising Sunset Boulevard or just watching the traffic. We sent one man up the canyon to the Country Store.

My best tail man was a big guy named John Eppick. He was a fearless wheel man who seldom lost a subject, and did a hell of a job for us. And I must modestly say, he was as good as me!

Eppick was as gung-ho as they come and had just bought a brand-new Dodge wagon with a big V-8. He had Betty riding with him and Maria was with me.

I was in the Arco station at Sunset and Fairfax paying the attendant for a tankful when Eppick's voice crackled over the CB:

"I got him. He's just turned off the Strip headed north towards Laurel Canyon."

What Eppick didn't mention was that as he spoke, he had been heading south on Crescent Heights and he proceeded to make a U-turn in the center of Crescent Heights and Sunset, without benefit of a green signal. I peeled out of the

Arco in my Buick, zipped north one block to Hollywood Blvd and hung a left a couple blocks to where Hollywood hit Crescent Heights as it turned into Laurel Canyon. I grabbed the mike and asked, "Where is he?" Eppick replied, "You're right along-side him." After a gulp, I looked to my left and sure as hell, there was Decatur's rented heap.

The street narrowed to one lane as we proceeded slowly up the canyon. Both Eppick and I tried frantically to raise some-one on the CB's who could pass the word that we had him and alert the coppers. I wanted them to make the arrest. But alas, as we feared, the canyon walls would only let Eppick and me talk to each other. I dropped behind Decatur and Eppick was behind me. We passed Mulholland and start-ed down the other side. I told Eppick to drop Betty off at Ventura and have her make the calls. But Eppick didn't want to miss the action and Betty nearly tumbled getting out as he roared back behind me again.

A few blocks north of Ventura, we passed a black and white going the opposite direction. I radioed Eppick to flag him down and he flipped another U-turn and disappeared. About two blocks later, Decatur made a left off of Laurel Canyon down a quiet, tree lined street where he pulled to the curb, turned off the lights and started to get out. Eppick and the cavalry were nowhere in sight and the radio didn't raise him. I slipped from behind the wheel and told Maria to drive to a pay phone and call the cops with our location.

Meanwhile, Decatur retrieved his daughter from the back seat. She appeared to be asleep. He carried her to a fourplex

apartment where he entered. I could see the little boy sleeping on the back seat.

Soon Decatur reappeared walking towards his car. Now
it was just him and me on a dark street. I reached his car
before he did and blocked the back door. Decatur's pace
slowed as he took in my movements. I called him by name
and told him not to open the car. He broke out into a big
grin and reached for the door handle. Now was the time . .
. the moment I was apprehensive about.

I said, "I've got a warrant Decatur, you're under arrest." He
said, "Yeah, well just let me get my boy out of the car and we
can talk." I pushed his arm back from the door handle – my
adrenalin was pumping as I braced for whatever he had. I
hoped he wasn't packing.

But the attack never came. Instead, he started backing up
and then turned and strolled back to the apartment. I knew
his little girl was in the apartment and the boy was in the car
next to me. What should I do? Before I figured that one out,
Maria drove up and I told her the situation.

As I finished, a black and white patrol car immediately
drove up. Maria showed the two officers the flyer we had
printed with Decatur's picture and the warrant information. This took some time. Then, as we all started towards
the apartment, another black and white showed up and we
had to tell the story again finishing as a third patrol car arrived with a skeptical sergeant who had to ponder our flyer
and story in detail. You could tell he was nervous about an

out-of-town warrant for child stealing. But Maria was persuasive. Unfortunately, more time was going by.

Finally, the six policemen, Maria and I entered the vestibule of the building. This was one of those two up and two down fourplexes. As the lead officer knocked on the door I looked around and saw all six were standing there with Maria and me. I asked if anyone was covering the back. The coppers looked at me quizzically as the door was opened by a female. Needless to say, by this time, Decatur and the little girl were gone. I barged past the cops towards the street and Decatur's car. It was still there and the little boy was asleep on the back seat. The cops fanned out, but Decatur was nowhere to be found. They took custody of the boy and the car which they ultimately discovered had some dope in the trunk. Maria and I drove to a pay phone to tell the answering service he had given us the slip.

Meanwhile, Eppick had his own problems, and this is what I later learned happened:

When he flipped the U-turn on Laurel Canyon, he caught the black and white and it pulled over. The officer went along with Eppick's excited plea for help after having the flyer and felony poop flashed at him. Eppick, however, was bent on catching up to me on Laurel Canyon, not knowing that I was now on a side street. The policeman was not fast enough for Eppick who took the lead instead of letting the patrol car with red lights and siren get in front. The further they went without seeing me, the faster Eppick drove.

At Oxnard Blvd. the light was a bit pink as Eppick came through. A fellow in a big 88 Oldsmobile headed westbound on Oxnard was waiting for the light to turn and when it did, he gunned it. Eppick's big Dodge T-boned the Oldsmobile, and his knee took out the CB radio as his car began to spin. The gas tank came off the Olds and ruptured spreading flaming fuel across the intersection. Eppick's Dodge continued to spin, shearing-off a fire hydrant which flooded the street and extinguished the flames. The black and white skidded into the intersection with red light and siren still going, barely stopping in time to miss the wreckage. This time Eppick had to admit he'd lost them.

As Maria and I made the call to the answering service, we saw a tow truck driving by with a familiar figure in the passenger seat and what was left of his Dodge on the hook. Eppick got out when he saw my car and we compared notes. At least we had the little boy but I should have known that Decatur was ruthless enough to leave one child and run with the other. I was kicking myself for not grabbing him when I had the chance.

In addition to his girlfriend in Studio City, Decatur had one in Laurel Canyon as well. When he ran from the apartment, he somehow got to a pay phone and called for a ride. His friend picked him and the little girl up and drove back into Laurel Canyon. They stopped at the little Canyon Store to get some milk for the girl.

Standing in front of the store, as per our evening's game plan, was Fred, the only one of our operatives who owned a pair of handcuffs. This fellow, a former Alcohol Beverage Control investigator, even had a handcuff tie-tack which many coppers wear as if they can't recognize each other any other way. Fred arrested Decatur and also cuffed him before Decatur knew what was happening. Fred made a call to LAPD, and the LAPD soon arrived and collected Decatur and the little girl.

After we picked Betty up at Ventura, Maria called the answering service to learn our disaster had turned to triumph. Maria called the mother and grandfather and they rushed down from Bakersfield while Maria convinced the LAPD to let her take the little boy to the West Hollywood Sheriff's station to join with the little girl and to meet their mother and grandfather.

Instead of getting a medal, we still had trouble collecting our bill from that old oil-driller hard case. Maria is retired, John Eppick has his own successful agency. For a number of years, John specialized in recovering stolen planes from Mexico. Fred faded away and Betty passed away a few years ago. I wonder where Decatur is?

ASPARAGUS

I have never cared for asparagus. And I don't understand fondness for prosciutto.

When I accepted the employment offer in 1960 at Krout and Schneider for $1.50 per hour, it's safe to say I was moderately desperate. But money didn't improve remarkably until I got into management. The HUSH case for Pacific Bell allowed us to greatly expand our staff in Los Angeles, while Northern California stayed about the same.

Tiring of the Santa Ana Freeway commute, we had moved from Cypress to Mt. Olympus in the Hollywood Hills in 1974 which put us closer to our sailboat in Marina del Rey. I took up scuba diving and underwater photography and we took my parents to Maui and Kuai two or three times and ultimately, several times to Kona.

I lunched once per week with lawyer and pal Dick Oshman who gave me a lot of free advice. I mentioned that although I owned about 25% of our company, I felt that since Southern California was now contributing more than 65% of the company's income, I would feel more comfortable with a little more ownership. He suggested I offer to buy some additional shares from Krout & Schneider's president and majority stockholder. I told him I had little cash. He said, "What about refinancing that Mt Olympus palace," which had appreciated a bunch?

Recently, I had graduated from a management course and one of my classmates was a VP with my mortgage lender. After a look-.see, he said the most his bank could loan was $72,000. So, I took it. When I met with the president in San Francisco he declined to sell as much stock as I wanted. But he did sell me about $10,000 worth and was surprised that I had the money to pay cash.

The Recession was well underway in the late 1970s. Now, I had $60k in the bank earning 3% on which I was paying 9.5% interest. There was little available to invest in during a real estate boom and one suggestion was buying houses in Hemet . . . *Geez.* My recent stock purchase made me about a 33% owner of the company, but the interest rates from inflation were killing me.

It was 1977 and we had made a date to meet scuba diving pals Peter and Linda in Kona. She was a School Superintendent, so wanted to go over during the Easter vacation. Marcia and I preferred an extra week, so we had our travel agent book us into hotels on Maui for the first week and find us a nice condo for four in Kona for the second week.

We played golf every day on Maui and shared Mai Tais with different couples after each round. Amazingly, more than one couple told us they had purchased condos in a lottery that weren't built yet, and in two cases, sold those unbuilt condos for a profit on Agreements of Sale. The real estate boom that had been going on in California had reached

Maui. Buying and then selling one that hadn't been built yet seemed crazy.

In Kona, we arrived a few hours before our friends and checked into the condo at Kona Bali Kai. Unlike most ocean front complexes, Bali Kai was built parallel to the beach, instead of perpendicular. All the units were ocean front. It was orgasmic. Our two bedroom-two bath was unit 310.

There was a little real estate shack next to one end of the building. I leaned in the door and asked if some of these units were for sale. The agent was reading a book. When he looked at my stringy cut-offs, tattoos and tank top topped by an old, stained tennis hat, he seemed annoyed I was bothering his reading.

His name was Wally Lentz, husband of the broker Lil Lentz. He grudgingly agreed to show me a unit on the fourth and top floor. When he told me he had six still for sale and the price was $92,600 each, requiring $10,000 down and $5,000 for a furniture package to put it in the rental program, I realized the Maui real estate boom had not yet reached Kona. We stood at the railing in unit 410, as I stared at the pounding surf, Wally was shuffling his feet and anxious to get back to his book. He said, "What's on your mind McClain?" I replied, "I'll tell you Wally, I'm just trying to figure if I should buy one of these or two of these." Wally's attitude changed immediately, and he showed me unit 422. I excused myself to get my check book, and quickly put the down payment on unit 410.

When I told Marcia, she was more than a little surprised and questioning my sanity. Our friends Peter and Linda soon arrived and agreed with her as we swilled down our Mai Tais. I had a restless night because I was worried about missing the beautiful oceanfront views if I sold unit 410. Bright and early at 9 a.m. the next morning, I met with Wally and also bought the other unit 422.

We flew back to the mainland and then gathered up my parents and flew back to Kona. They helped us pick out furniture and wall hangings for both the units, which was fun.

A few months later, the phone rang, and it was realtor Lil Lentz. She was worried I still had some money left and informed me that the real estate boom had finally reached Kona. She said a new project called Keahou Punahele was under construction in Kaanapali, and they were now having lotteries. If interested, we needed to send a cashier's check for $10,000 to enter the lottery for a unit that was on a golf course with the ocean on the other side of the fairway.

After I sent my check, I mentioned it to John Staley, an old scheming pirate friend, and he also sent a check. We both won the lottery and bought golf course facing apartments with stunning ocean views. A few weeks after we and the Staley's occupied our units, without telling me, Staley bought another unit that was next-door to mine. That really annoyed me, so without mentioning it to Staley, Buck and I bought a unit on the other side of Staley's which gave us one on each side of his. We all got some laughs out of that. John and Louise were dear friends and Marcia and Louise stayed in Punahele together when John and I had to go back to the mainland to work.

As nearly a year went by, Lil Lentz informed me that a well-off farmer from Iowa wanted to buy our unit 422 because his wife was driving him nuts since she had vacationed in our rental. His offers kept increasing. When we passed the one-year mark to achieve long term capital gains, I sold unit 422 to him for $187,000. A nice return on less than twenty thousand invested. Today they are selling for over $500k.

A year or three later, we called Lil to let her know we were coming to Kona for a visit. I guess she thought we were good customers having bought four condos. Lil wanted to do something special for dinner on their lanai, so after great shopping difficulty she served us an appetizer of asparagus wrapped in prosciutto followed by an entrée featuring . . . ASPARAGUS.

GENE AUTRY and the UNITED STATES MARINES

From 1988 to 2003 we lived in Fallbrook, California, and raised avocados on 500 trees. Which, next to owning a race-horse, is one of the best ways I know to lose money. Our small North San Diego County community backed up to the U.S. Marine base at Camp Pendleton, one of the largest Marine bases in the country. Many Marine families lived in Fallbrook. Concomitantly, I ran the San Diego branch of Krout & Schneider, Inc. for several years. In 2003 we moved to the desert to Indio which is centered in the Coachella Valley near Palm Springs.

I learned about a woman named Erica Stone who had formed a charitable organization named Soldiers Organized Services, and went by the acronym, S.O.S. This started when Erica had met a Marine at the Palm Springs Airport who had missed the last bus to Twenty-Nine Palms where the largest Marine base in the country, geographically, is located. Cab fare between the airport and base is usually between $150 and $200. She drove him up there that night.

After seeing a newspaper article about S.O.S, I looked her up and for nine years became one of the volunteer drivers, mostly old veterans like myself, who provided free transportation. From my home in Indio to the base and back via the Palm Springs International Airport is 168 miles for which the IRS generously allowed me 14 cents per mile off my taxes. Since 2007, S.O.S has moved tens of thousands of Marines, usually over 1,500 at Christmas alone, sometimes with their little families. Using donation money, Erica rents busses to augment the volunteer drivers in their personal vehicles. Jacqueline "Jackie" Autry, widow of cowboy movie star and businessman, Gene Autry, lives in Palm Springs. Mrs. Autry is one of the most generous donors to S.O.S who with help from the local Chrysler dealer has also given several vans to S.O.S.

The major domo of this operation is a piece of work. Watching Erica load five busses with Marines and their luggage would be a good way to train drill sergeants. She is in charge.

In my Traverse my usual load is three to four Marines. We pick them up at the USO, who incidentally also should have a special place in heaven awaiting them. The USO volunteers host and feed the Marines providing sleeping quarters and a place for their gear.

I don't like to compete with cell phones when driving, so I request that the Marines put them away when they ride with me. As soon as we start out, I ask them if they know who Gene Autry was. Most of these young men and women don't, so I explain he was a singing cowboy movie star who didn't waste his money on booze and dope but bought radio and TV stations. Then I ask if any of them know when television was invented. Same answer. I explain first televisions were available to the public in 1947. Now, we are reaching the intersection with Gene Autry Trail, a sign that impresses them. I ask if they ever heard the song, "Here Comes Santa Claus," they all have, so I explain:

Gene Autry was the Grand Marshall of the Santa Claus Lane Parade on Hollywood Boulevard in 1946 preceding the Santa Claus float. The kids were all screaming "here come Santa Claus" and not "here comes Gene Autry." On the way home he said to his then wife Ina Mae, "That's a great idea for a song." And that very night he sat down and wrote the lyrics to "Here Comes Santa Claus." Oakley Haldeman later wrote the melody.

On Monday, Gene called his producer and told him he had an idea for a song to record and would need another song for the other side of the record. When the producer called back, he said he had a song, but it had kind of a goofy name. Gene liked it and so for the other side of the record he recorded "Rudolph the Red Nosed Reindeer." It sold two and one-half million the first year and over 25,000,000 as the second best-selling record of all time until the 1980's.

Gene Autry also founded the Los Angeles Angels baseball team in 1961, which moved to Anaheim in 1966 and was later named the Anaheim Angels. My wife Marcia saw his limo bearing an "Angels" license plate more than once on the Santa Ana Freeway. And there was Gene in his cowboy hat riding in the back seat, and he always had a friendly wave and a tip of the hat.

PUNITIVE DAMAGES
May 1, 2022

Today, the jury returned a verdict in the Johnny Depp vs Amber Heard case. Before the verdict was issued, the announcer made some mention of the different types of damages that could result. One is actual damages and the other is punitive damages.

In our business, being sued occasionally, goes with the territory. As a result, it was critical that we have a multi-million-dollar Comprehensive General Liability policy, usually, with our client named as additional insureds on the policy. I learned right away that these policies do not cover punitive damages. The reason being, as the name implies, these damages are intended to be punitive and therefore cannot legally be insured against.

Almost every time our firm was sued for actual damages, the plaintiffs also asked for punitive damages. When the plaintiff won or it was settled, the insurance company lawyers always got the plaintiff to drop the punitive cause of action. On only one occasion, did we lose a case where punitive damages were assessed. It was also one of the rare times that our case went to verdict and was not settled by our insurance carrier in advance.

I don't remember our code name for the case, but I'll call the client Ajax Rubber Inc. This division manufactured sporting goods such as basketballs, golf clubs, etc. They were losing a lot of products out the back door of their huge Orange County warehouse. We put undercover operatives on all three shifts and augmented with surveillance as necessary. We found a number of warehouse employees taking product out to their cars.

This lawsuit stemmed from the conductor of a freight train who we caught receiving stolen product from his pals in the warehouse. We even had film of this train company employee putting the stolen stuff into the trunk of his car after he finished his shift on the train.

We covered some Orange County bars where our client's stuff was being sold by various warehouse employees. We made a very substantial number of undercover buys to the point where one 8 x 10 room of our Santa Ana office was nearly full of evidence.

When I went to the Orange County Sheriff's they were not hot about getting involved with a complicated case. Ditto for the District Attorney, but the DA finally convinced the Sheriff to make some arrests and insisted I immediately provide them with a detailed inventory of the evidence we had recovered. I assigned one of our best guys, Eli Chavira, to knock out the inventory in a hurry, preparatory to returning all the contraband to our client when the case was over.

One of the people arrested was the train conductor which should have been a slam dunk considering our photographic evidence. But his criminal case came to trial the day before Christmas and the DA sent a green horn Deputy DA because everyone was off or partying. The inexperienced lawyer failed to obtain a stipulation to probable cause for the arrest. In the Christmas spirit, (and to shorten his holiday calendar) the criminal judge let the thief go, though the railroad (also one of our clients) had fired him.

After nearly a year, he sued us for various issues included losing his job and asked for punitive damages as well as the actual damages. It took a considerable time (nearly two years as I recall) for this lawsuit to make its way through the legal red tape until it finally came to trial. Our insurance carrier was the famous British Lloyds of London, which in itself was unusual. I appeared on behalf of Krout & Schneider.

The client's representative was a man I'll call Mr. Gruff. Mr. Gruff was about to retire at the time he hired us and now he had to interrupt his retirement. He had supervised their end of the investigations when he was the head of Human Resources for Ajax. He was a short-tempered old man who did not suffer fools, though I always got along with him. He was really annoyed at having to appear at this trial for something that happened two years ago and was encroaching on his private time.

At the trial, our attorney, a quiet, competent defense lawyer, would stand up and recite the facts which to me seemed incontrovertible. The plaintiff's lawyer on the other hand was the exact opposite. He was animated, verbose, and very accusatory. Out of whole cloth, he fashioned a conspiracy between my company and Ajax, of which his client, the former train conductor, was the victim. He made Mr. Gruff angry and defensive on the stand which helped his theory that we had conspired against his client. Adding to this was my being technically impeached for the first and only time of well over one hundred court appearances.

As I was testifying, the plaintiff's lawyer, who I'll call Mr. Darrow, stood holding a sheaf of papers several feet away from the witness box and asked if I recognized it. I asked him to come closer. Still at some distance, I could see my signature at the bottom of Krout & Schneider letterhead. I insisted he let me look at the package of papers which appeared to be copies of an inventory.

The cover letter addressed to the DA was signed by me stating in summary, "Here is the inventory." The inventory was on plain white paper. Every report my company renders is always on legal paper with the lines numbered and it's always typed on an electric typewriter. So, I testified that while I recognized the cover letter, the other papers were unfamiliar to me. I testified that the papers did appear to be the inventory of stolen goods. I had forgotten that the secretaries in our Santa Ana office were jammed with work when Eli Chavira was preparing the inventory, so as an expedient for an anxious District Attorney, Eli had typed the inventory on his own portable typewriter on plain bond paper.

Mr. Darrow didn't allow me to correct my testimony but made several accusatory statements saying that this was proof of the conspiracy between Krout & Schneider and Ajax, to persecute his client.

Meanwhile, our defense lawyer continued to stand rather quietly, recite the facts and irrelevance of what Mr. Darrow was saying, before sitting down. The jury was buying Darrow's performance hook, line, and sinker and ignoring what our lawyer said in defense. The clincher was Mr. Darrow holding up the lack of a criminal conviction by the DA, as proof he was not guilty. We lost the verdict.

On damages, the jury awarded the plaintiff $15,000 in actual damages which even in those days was not a great deal and was paid by our insurance company. But to punish us for conspiring against this poor plaintiff, they awarded him $5,000 in punitive damages. Of course, Lloyds of London reminded us they did not cover punitive. So much for justice.

THE VINDICTIVE THIEVES

Our client was perplexed. This major wholesaler of household appliances was being stolen blind. They hired a new supervisor to crack down on procedures. He made some progress and some enemies. He quit when someone fired a shotgun at the front door of his home.

There were only vague suspicions, but the client suspected most problems involved the third shift. We canvassed swap meets and found several booths that offered our client's products, still new in the box. But the identification on the boxes and products could not be tied to inventory from our client's warehouse.

We videotaped the vendors, followed them home and identified them. Although none were on our client's payroll, investigation and surveillance soon tied them to some of our client's current employees. But we had to perfect the chain of evidence, and placed an undercover operative in the client's warehouse.

After four weeks, our undercover operative was taken into confidence by the thieves. They continued a methodical pilfering of as much as pallet loads. But this time our operative marked the outgoing loot with an invisible marking pen. He soon learned the identity of truck drivers who assisted the warehouse thieves.

Our surveillance team videotaped the truckers dropping off product at the garages of the swap-meet vendors. Investigators, posing as customers, purchased the goods at the swap meets. Our black light kit revealed the initials and dates marked on the goods by our operative. This was the proof we needed to create the chain of evidence.

We never learned who fired the shotgun, but interviews led to confessions and terminations. Our client cleaned house and the bottom line improved considerably.

DEADWEIGHT EMPLOYMENT CONTRACTS

A conglomerate was in trouble. They had acquired several diverse companies and given generous contract incentives to the entrepreneur owners who now became part of the conglomerate.

Now, two of the new divisions were mysteriously under-performing and the salaries paid to the division presidents were out of line. We investigated using all of our tools.

Though difficult to manipulate the hiring process, we were able to place an undercover operative in key locations at both companies. Having inside intelligence allowed us to minimize the surveillance necessary to tie all of the pieces together.

One division president had furtively started a competing business in violation of his contract. He set up a puppet management that allowed him to call the shots, but remain behind the scene.

The other president conspired with a competitor while bleeding his former brainchild. His ownership interest in the competing company was even recorded in public documents. In both cases, surveillance to document secret meetings with co-conspirators provided the missing links to the other evidence.

Key admissions during interviews of both suspect and friendly witnesses provided conclusive corroboration. Our client terminated the culprits, voiding their contracts and restored the companies to a profit-making mode. Hundreds of thousands of dollars were saved by proving the facts.

Before There Was ENRON . . .
there was this guy

THE CASE OF: IF IT'S TOO GOOD TO BE TRUE . . .

The call came from an out-of-state investment advisor. Although he was positive this was a wonderful deal for his clients, could we do a limited due diligence inquiry to verify an investment was sound? His authorization was limited, but he forwarded the sales propaganda and two home-made financial statements from the subject who we will call Tom Cromwell. He said Cromwell indicated there would soon be an audited financial statement from a Big Five accounting firm.

Cromwell claimed to be in the business of factoring accounts receivable for doctors with cash-flow problems. He would buy insurance claims from the doctors for 80 cents on the dollar, collect from the insurance company and make 20% profit. If the claim was not collected within 90 days, the doctor had to buy it back. In this way, Cromwell claimed to recirculate investors' money three or four times during a year generating huge profits of 30 to 40 percent annually.

Cromwell's Newport Beach office was a showplace. He drove a Rolls Royce, collected vintage autos and his office walls were covered with ostensibly valuable art. He claimed he had several expensive homes. His bank, a big one, loved him. But why would doctors discount their bills 20% instead of waiting 90 days for payment? Public records were clean. No criminal record or serious civil problems. We had used up our authorization, but our curiosity dictated spending our own money to look further.

Our contact with the Big Five accounting firm said Cromwell was not a client, but a call to the local partner revealed he had been lunching Cromwell, whose office was in their building, and been stalled for months about getting his account for an audit. We called a contact, Chief Auditor for a top banking client. He agreed to try Cromwell's bank through the back door. When he did, he was told Cromwell was gold-plated. The SEC refused to provide information, but hinted they had an open file. LAPD Organized Crime unit was mum.

We report facts, not opinions. We were forced to report no evidence of wrongdoing, but cautioned our client as strongly as we dared about the business premise and reluctance to sign up for the audit. Our client ignored our advice and issued this statement to his clients:

"Only rarely does something that seems too good to be true turn out to be true. This is one of those rare exceptions . . . Let me state as a bonded investment advisor: 'Of everything I have investigated for my clients at any time, this is the absolute <u>best</u> high return investment I have <u>ever</u> seen for a combination of safety, liquidity and return.'"

Three months later, the SEC indictment said Cromwell had fleeced nearly a thousand clients for over $10,000 each. A classic Ponzi scheme paying off old investors with new investors' funds.

But the irony came four months later when our Chief Bank Auditor client called. "Hi Ed, you remember the favor I did for you on Tom Cromwell?" "Yes," we said. "Well, I neglected to check our own records. He took us for $52,000."

BANK FRAUD

In the early 1970's, one of California's larger banks set up a special unit to handle mortgage banking. It had $200 million to lend out to qualified home buyers.

The bank put a newly-made hotshot senior vice president in charge but installed very little oversight to check up on what the unit was doing. A flamboyant mortgage broker established a relationship with the vice president. The new unit started to package multi-dollar mega-deals.

Normally, mortgage loans that are being applied for, require an independent appraisal of the collateral. The properties are evaluated to be sure the loan to value ratio protects the bank. The mortgage broker convinced the vice president he could provide a one-stop service.

Instead of hiring independent appraisers, the mortgage broker would provide the appraisals. The vice president was pleased because now, the deals were going through much faster since they didn't have to wait for the independent appraisals.

What's more, the assessed value was always as high or higher than the borrower needed to get the loan approved. When the internal bank auditors get wind of the situation, it looked like the bank had lost tens of thousands.

The bank called us in to develop hidden assets of the mortgage broker and of the vice president. The bank wanted to know if the two had colluded together to defraud the bank. If they found collusion, the bank would sue to attempt to recover damages.

Our investigation finds a lot of information and some assets, but the banker looks like he may have been conned.

The bank quietly transfers, then fires him. The bank is reluctant to admit their stupidity and they try to keep a lid on the whole mess. The Wall Street Journal picks up the thread, but never gives it much play. It is more convenient for the bankers not to have the unfavorable publicity. They make little recovery and the matter dies.

The bank is overloaded with legitimate non-performing real estate loans in addition to this bunch. They merge with a bigger bank and lay off hundreds.

THE MILLION DOLLAR JUROR

A runaway $45,000,000 verdict. Our client needed some basis for a new trial. They had only a few days to file a motion.

A poll of the jury revealed a juror confided his criminal record to a fellow panelist. When contacted, he clammed up. We needed the facts fast. His background included residencies in several other states going back thirty years. The record keeping in those states was manual and haphazard.

At a county seat in the Deep South, a dusty volume atop an unused shelf revealed the juror's name with no details. But we found the answer at the State Prison on a 3 x 5 index card kept in a recipe box . . . three years served for a felony. It was him. And he had lied on his jury questionnaire.

My long-time investigator friend in Jackson, Mississippi, called to say that a law office in his building had asked him to do the same investigation as I had. I asked my friend to let me know the results first since I had given him the job first. It appeared that my Los Angeles client was playing it safe by hiring a back-up investigation.

Our client's motion for a new trial was granted and a much-reduced award negotiated which saved our client's bacon. And Krout & Schneider's reputation for results in a hurry was intact.

THE GANG-BANGING DOPE DEALERS

Decisions that came back to haunt. As a cost-cutting move, this major distributor/wholesaler tried to save money by not screening applicants for employment. To cut down on the expense of help-wanted ads and personnel processing, they also encouraged employees to recommend friends and relatives for employment. A good idea if your employees aren't crooks. But in this case . . . a fateful combination.

Soon the workforce had a high percentage of gang members. The initial hires brought in their homies. Inventory losses increased exponentially. Supervisors, co-workers and human resource personnel were intimidated.

It should have been obvious that drugs were being used, bought and sold on the premises. For a time, the company ignored the abuse of sick benefits, absenteeism, skyrocketing work comp claims from hot-dog accidents with fork lifts and a general loss of productivity.

Finally, upper management was confronted by a half-dozen honest employees who opened their eyes, though insisted they did not wish to become involved. The company's labor lawyer recommended Krout & Schneider.

We placed undercover operatives on all three shifts. Acceptance by gang bangers did not come easy, but eventually we developed relationships with the bad guys. With no fear of being caught, they continued to use dope and pilfer product with impunity.

We established liaison with law enforcement to facilitate purchase and booking of controlled substances as evidence. The authorities agreed to let us finish our investigation and interviews before moving on the major dope dealers. We purchased and booked small quantities of cocaine and marijuana to avoid arousing suspicion, but we learned and reported that larger quantities were being sold.

After six months of fact gathering, we kicked off the interviews with a bust of several pallet loads of product being purloined in a conspiracy with shippers. The Sheriff was happy to assist.

Gang members are not an easy interview and the confession rate drops, but we had good success considering many had criminal records. We faked interviews of our undercover operatives so as not to blow their cover. Sufficient evidence was obtained to sustain multiple terminations. The client chose to discipline and place the minor drug abusers on probation. Many employees came forth and commended management for finally taking these actions.

As a postscript: Six months after the completion of our work, the client called to advise the drop in their shrinkage had more than paid for our investigation. They said worker's comp claims were down and absenteeism was negligible. And now *Smart*HIRE screens every new hire.

Krout & Schneider, Inc. *When you need to know beyond a reasonable doubt.*

KNUTE

In the many years that I have been investigating suspected insurance fraud, I have seen a few genuinely injured and disabled claimants. The number is very small compared to the overall number of cases assigned to me, and for good reason. Insurance companies seldom assign cases for investigation unless there are a number of signs which point to the possibility of malingering. Sub-rosa investigation is expensive, so the bulk of the ten percent or so of cases which are thoroughly investigated, involve claimants who are exaggerating or outright faking their claims of injury.

In almost every case, I have found insurance companies are grateful to learn when their suspicions are unfounded and they are dealing with a legitimate claim. Usually, they make an effort to settle the case, rather than fight it. Unfortunately, the primary flaw in our system is that malingerers are often paid off because it is cheaper to settle the case than to investigate and litigate. This merely encourages more illegitimate claims.

A memorable case involved a man past middle age who was pinned between a semi-trailer and a loading dock, receiving crushing injuries to his pelvic area. When I reviewed my client's file, the medical portion reflected genuine injuries and serious medical treatment over several years. The file was thick and the claim was dragging on, as far as the insurance company was concerned. Their doctor was reluctant to declare the claimant's condition "permanent and stationary" (a term they use). Unlike most files I review, the claimant, who I will call Knute, had never sought a lawyer. His treating physician was the insurance company's own choice, a respected surgeon. That is one reason the carrier didn't press for a conclusion.

Somehow, the insurance claims examiner suddenly discovered that the address to which he was mailing disability checks, was in fact, the residence address of the treating physician. This alarmed the carrier since the doctor had never disclosed anything other than a doctor-patient relationship and he continued to certify Knute's temporary disability.

The doctor's residence turned out to be an estate of several acres, located on a hill overlooking a city seventy miles east of Los Angeles. A large two-story home with a long driveway dominated the pinnacle and the grounds fell away towards the city in a dense combination of mature fruit and ornamental trees. There were outbuildings which I suspected could house servants. It was impossible to drive or walk up to the estate and comprehend the property. I was not sure where the doctor's property ended on the down side since there was no fence or markers. I was concerned about trespass, but felt the situation was questionable enough to warrant a closer look.

I parked my vehicle well away and below the property, and trekked up the hill into the trees carrying binoculars, a triple turret 16mm camera and another with a 14-inch lens which could film identifiable activity from a quarter mile away. I had several boxes of film, a pillow to rest my camera and my lunch. It was about 6 A.M. sometime around 1962.

I was picking my way through the trees trying to make as little noise as possible in the dry leaves. Suddenly, I was confronted by a large stooped and weathered looking man with a surprisingly friendly attitude, given the circumstance. I suspected immediately he was my subject. He did not seem annoyed or suspicious but just curious. He easily accepted I was a GI Bill student from the local college on a bird watching expedition. He seemed pleased to have company and told me I had come to the right place because he had plenty of birds. He led me to a series of pens which contained some birds but the amazing thing were the birds outside of the cages. The place was like a game preserve and the various fowl, which included Hungarian partridge, quail and pheasant were walking about with impunity.

I was obliged to shoot some film of the birds after Knute confirmed his identity. We settled in as the morning mist receded into beautiful sunshine. Knute left to get some beverages and came back with fresh fruit from the orchard. The more I looked at him, the more it was obvious that he was not just stooped, but rather bent over from the waist. He didn't volunteer anything about his injury initially, so I got him to tell me the story of his life.

As a younger man, he was originally a wrangler/stuntman who hooked up with the first motion picture studios. Those were the days of the silent film when movies were completed in a matter of days.

Knute rattled off the names of the famous directors and stars he had worked with even after talkies came along. He said he was one of the few wranglers who would do the stunt recognized as the most dangerous in films. Dropping off the lead horse of a six-horse team pulling a stagecoach and passing between the horses and the wheels. Sometimes he was garbed as an Indian and sometimes he was dressed like the star cowboy.

Knute served in the Army during WWII, but sort of drifted in the fifties and mumbled something about a wife and son long since departed. He had no family, no pension, and had picked up a day job unloading trucks, which was his undoing. He spoke in glowing terms about the doctor who had become interested in his story and offered him a position as caretaker on his estate. He was pleased to have a place to sleep and a ride downtown once a week for groceries. His prospects for recovery were limited but he was optimistic saying he had been banged up many times during his life and always bounced back. But to me, he looked hopelessly crippled.

I stayed with Knute until early afternoon when I excused myself and made my report. I phoned the boss to tell him I had two mags of film of birds, but none of the claimant. I suppose the doctor had a conflict of interest by taking in a patient he was treating, but I sure couldn't blame him. As with most cases, I never heard the outcome, but the claims examiner did ask to talk to me to be sure I wasn't going soft. I got the impression they were going to lean on the doctor for a final evaluation and then settle the case.

I wish my grandchildren could hear some of Knute's stories.

MISCELLANY

I assume some of the readers of this book will be uninitiated in the ways of investigation, so I will relate how it really goes down.

In the first place, the bulk of the field work I engaged in was done without divulging my identity and using a variety of subterfuges. It was seldom a case of displaying my ID and copping to my true purpose.

In all surveillance cases, concealing my identity was mandatory to having any success. It is not rocket science. Driving ability is important. Changing one's appearance is also needed from time to time and I had a few standard items that worked well for me. And I still recommend their use.

A hard hat. A lunch pail. Coveralls, preferably with some paint on them. I had an ancient wooden surveyor's tripod which I used often. I have entered construction sites following a malingering worker, hauled out my tripod, and filmed him by using my 14" camera atop the tripod in broad daylight for extended periods without raising attention. Workers don't talk to surveyors, nor understand them.

I have used the hard hat and coveralls and lunch box in many places, even in Beverly Hills. A high percentage of subterfuge contacts were done wearing the coveralls, before changing back to regular clothes for the remainder of the tail.

THE IMPORTANCE OF SURVEILLANCE

A couple of years or more ago I was at a meeting of PI's and I heard two guys pooh pooing surveillance investigators as not being as qualified as other specialties. Yet in nearly every heavyweight investigation related in this book, most could not have been accomplished without some surveillance to tie the bad guys together, usually at restaurants or businesses.

H.R.

Our company is famous for taking people with little experience and training them to do our work. Many were so successful that they went on to open their own agencies. For the first three years of my days with Krout & Schneider I did all the training in the Los Angeles office. I tried to wash out the losers as soon as possible.

One time, our manager hired a former pots and pans door to door salesman because he thought the guy would be good at subterfuge contacts. He failed to notice the glasses which looked like Coke bottle bottoms. His name was Sol.

He passed the first test by meeting me at 4:30 AM for breakfast. Our assignment was on 103rd Street in Watts, the heart of the later riots. Most of the lots in Watts are deep, often with three houses per lot. Since three families used every driveway, you had to be alert. I lectured him to watch the driveway and tell me when a vehicle came out. Soon, I saw a car exit the driveway and start towards our position. The car passed us and Sol didn't say a word. He was still staring at the drive. It was his last day. I had another guy named Sol who I told to bring his sack lunch because our job was in the wilds of rural Lancaster. After a few hours watching a farm house, I suggested we have lunch. Sol informed me he couldn't eat his lunch until he washed his hands as required by his faith. I felt sorry for him and drove four miles to the nearest Standard and fortunately our subject didn't come out until later.

Hiring friends doesn't always work out either. I had a buddy named Max. He was a cracker jack experimental machinist and because I had spoken so highly of my company and the work I was doing, he hounded me for a job. His last assignment was on a California Highway Patrol officer faking a back injury. When Max arrived in Fontana, he called the cops to let them know he was on surveillance. Soon, the big Chippy came out with two very large German Shepherds. He put them in the car and drove towards Max, flipped a U and pulled up behind Max's wheels. He let the dogs out then came to Max's window to talk. Max copped to his identity and even showed the highway patrolman his ID. The case was burned to a crisp, but had a happy ending after Max quit.

On Saturday, I loaded Marcia and my two boys Mark and Lee (aged about eight and five) and some kites and headed for Fontana. The CHP officer had a big open field behind his home. He was building a con-block back wall. He paid little attention to our feeble kite flying efforts because he had a forty-pound cement block in either hand and was intent on his work. We kept trying until a little breeze came up and I rested my camera on Marcia's shoulder while getting 250 feet of great 16 mm activity. Mark and Lee are the same two guys who now have over fifty-years PI experience each and run Krout & Schneider, Inc. but are no better at flying kites with my great-grandsons.

TROUBLE

PI work, except for the driving, is usually not dangerous. But there are exceptions like when a guy tried to slug me through a plate glass window after I served him a subpoena in front of Denny's. Another ended better than I hoped.

I had an overt assignment to interview and obtain a statement from a lady who lived on Vernon Ave (now Martin Luther King) across the street from a bar that LAPD would not enter with less than six cops. After my knock on the door, a woman who answered said my subject was not at home. I was just climbing down the steps when a man and woman came out of the bar and started happily towards me. I suspect they were both three sheets to the wind and from their hand holding I got the impression they might be planning some fun.

As they neared, the lady who fit the description of my subject seemed to notice my white face on her doorstep and started to frown. Her companion didn't see me at first, but also stopped smiling when he did. I asked her if she was Mrs. subject and she let go of her companion's hand, shook her head, then pushed past me and in the front door which she slammed, leaving her likely paramour on the sidewalk. He was obviously not happy. His face had what may have been a razor or knife scar, though I didn't stop to study it. From the steps I started towards my car some 60 yards away. I sensed he was following me.

I maintained a regular pace, but he was moving a little faster. Before I reached my car, I heard him say "Lumumba has the right idea, "they ought to kill all you white mother- - - ers." Then his hand grabbed me on my shoulder and started to spin me around. I don't remember what I said, but the way I said it seemed to surprise him and he didn't hold on to my shoulder, but kind of stopped in his tracks. After a pause, I reached my car and he walked back towards her house. I never saw a knife. All I had was a clip board.

For those of you who may not remember, Patrice Lumumba was the controversial Prime Minister of the newly formed, Republic of the Congo much in the news before his assassination in the days of waning African colonization.

WHY <u>YOU</u> NEED TO BELONG TO TRADE ASSOCIATIONS

by Eddy McClain CPI CII

Not having the benefits of belonging to a trade association, is like having one arm tied behind your back. Many of the reasons are not as obvious as others. You may not perceive their effect on your bottom line, but they are there.

They say the Boston Tea Party was about objecting to "taxation, without representation." But that essentially still goes on in our country and states when law makers make laws in a vacuum. Most of the time, when a bad law is enacted, it could have been stopped or modified by convincing the authors of its faults or unintended consequences.

But let's talk about the more tangible benefits of belonging:

A very experienced investigator commented, "In 60 years. I've never been to an association meeting where I either didn't learn something, or meet someone I could use as a resource . . . or both."

When I started in the business, my company advertised we covered the West Coast. To do that, we needed ten offices, some with only one or two employees. Now, trade association members can achieve instant, timely, competent results as near as their keyboard. The CALI Listserv is terrific for California assignments and NCISS's is outstanding for national work. And members can benefit from exchange work from fellow members. Once in a while it can be a large assignment, or one that keeps on giving for months. But if you don't belong to an association your company won't be in their directory and you won't know who the best agencies are to send your exchange assignments, either.

Getting back to bad laws that could be avoided: NCISS dodged a bullet for the profession when we testified before Congress and they enacted the DPPA. It took six years, but NCISS also fixed the Fair Credit Reporting Act which had screwed up employment investigations.

The European countries have recemtly enacted privacy laws that are a perfect example of what to guard against. You can bet the same will be tried in our legislatures too. The time to deal with these consequences is by supporting a group that will guard your flanks, in advance. You can't do much by yourself, but there is strength in numbers. Support your state association and the National Council of Investigation and Security Services, NCISS, with your membership.

The author is Chairman of Krout & Schneider, Inc. a 95-year-old investigation agency in California. He has served as President, Chairman, and Legislative Chair of both the California Association of Licensed Investigators, CALI, and the National Council of Investigation and Security Services, NCISS. He has testified before Congress four times leading up to the DPPA and FCRA exemptions for investigations.

HISTORY

Krout & Schneider, Inc. was founded on February 14, 1927 by J. Edward Krout and Sam A. Schneider. At the time, there were no professional investigation agencies as we know them today. So-called "detectives" were tough guys who packed guns and hung around the free lunch counter of the local saloon. They would collect a debt if persuasion were needed. Nearly everyone drove a black Ford.

Ed and Sam had the idea of a "white collar service" for business, law firms and insurance companies. There was a need, but they had barely started before the stock market crash of 1929 and the following Great Depression.

During much of the thirties, the Golden Gate and Oakland Bay bridges were under construction. Both construction companies were our clients. A worker injured on one bridge would often go to work on the other. In 1932, Schneider, a photography buff with his own darkroom, secured a commercial motion picture rig. He filmed a malingering claimant and motion picture evidence was admitted into court for the first time.

Needless to say, we have had many interesting cases. Chasing crooks and matching wits with fraudsters is hard work, but fun. And being asked for our input by attorneys and execs trying to solve a problem is rewarding too.

Today, K & S is still the leader in sub-rosa investigation, but we also specialize in employee misconduct investigations. Our undercover investigators and interviewers are the bane of thieves and drug dealers in the workplace.

Our pre-employment screening division, **SmartHIRE**, conducts background investigations nationally for all types and sizes of employers.

Ed Krout died in 1961, but Sam Schneider remained active with the firm until his death in 1986. Starting in the fifties, Ed and Sam began one of the first employee stock ownership programs, ensuring built-in continuity of management and excellence of service. Many of our employees have decades of experience and service. We are proud of our history and appreciate the loyalty of clients who have trusted us for almost a century.

J. Edward Krout
1898-1961

Sam A. Schneider
1898-1986

Printed in the USA
CPSIA information can be obtained
at www.ICGtesting.com
CBHW071311150324
5426CB00012B/998